S250 Science in Context
Science: Level 2

The Open University

TOPIC 4
Medicinal plants

Prepared for the Course Team by Michael Gillman

This publication forms part of the Open University course S250 *Science in Context*. Details of this and other Open University courses can be obtained from the Student Registration and Enquiry Service, The Open University, PO Box 197, Milton Keynes, MK7 6BJ, United Kingdom: tel. +44 (0)845 300 6090, email general-enquiries@open.ac.uk

Alternatively, you may visit the Open University website at http://www.open.ac.uk where you can learn more about the wide range of courses and packs offered at all levels by The Open University.

To purchase a selection of Open University course materials visit http://www.ouw.co.uk, or contact Open University Worldwide, Michael Young Building, Walton Hall, Milton Keynes MK7 6AA, United Kingdom for a brochure. tel. +44 (0)1908 858785; fax +44 (0)1908 858787; email ouwenq@open.ac.uk

The Open University
Walton Hall, Milton Keynes
MK7 6AA

First published 2006. Second edition 2007.

Edited and designed by The Open University.

Typeset by The Open University.

Printed and bound in the United Kingdom by The University Press, Cambridge.

ISBN 978 0 7492 1889 8

2.1

The S250 Course Team

Andrew J. Ball (*Author, Topic 2*)

John Baxter (*Author, Topic 6*)

Steve Best (*Media Developer*)

Kate Bradshaw (*Multimedia Producer*)

Audrey Brown (*Associate Lecturer and Critical Reader*)

Mike Bullivant (*Course Manager*)

James Davies (*Media Project Manager*)

Steve Drury (*Author, Topic 3*)

Lydia Eaton (*Media Assistant*)

Chris Edwards (*Course Manager*)

Mike Gillman (*Author, Topic 4*)

Debbie Gingell (*Course Assistant*)

Sara Hack (*Media Developer*)

Sarah Hofton (*Media Developer*)

Martin Keeling (*Media Assistant*)

Richard Holliman (*Course Themes and Author, Topic 1*)

Jason Jarratt (*Media Developer*)

Simon P. Kelley (*Author, Topic 2*)

Nigel Mason (*Topic 7*)

Margaret McManus (*Media Assistant*)

Elaine McPherson (*Course Manager*)

Pat Murphy (*Course Team Chair and Author, Topic 1*)

Judith Pickering (*Media Project Manager*)

William Rawes (*Media Developer*)

Shelagh Ross (*Author, Topic 7*)

Sam Smidt (*Author, Topic 7*)

Valda Stevens (*Learning Outcomes and Assessment*)

Margaret Swithenby (*Media Developer*)

Jeff Thomas (*Author, Topics 6 and 7*)

Pamela Wardell (*Media Developer*)

Kiki Warr (*Author, Topic 5*)

The Course Team would like to thank the following for their particular contributions: Benny Peiser (*Liverpool John Moores University; Author, Topic 2*), David Bard (*Associate Lecturer; Author, Topic 6*) and Barbara Brockbank (*Associate Lecturer; Author, Topic 6 and Critical Reader*).

Dr Jon Turney (*University College London and Imperial College London*) was External Assessor for the course. The External Assessors for individual topics were: Professor John Mann (*Queen's University, Belfast*); Professor John McArthur (*University College London*); Dr Richard Reece (*University of Manchester*); Dr Rosalind M. Ridley (*University of Cambridge*); Dr Duncan Steel (*Macquarie University, Australia*); Dr David Viner (*University of East Anglia*) and Professor Mark Welland FRS (*University of Cambridge*).

Contents

Silphion: the birth control drug of the Ancient Greeks

In this topic, we will discuss how people have discovered, utilised and researched plants with medicinal properties. Medicinal plants have been used for thousands of years and represent complex interactions between past and present science and culture. Through examples of observation and experiment in natural environments and the laboratory you will explore the scientific study of medicinal plants, providing many links to all of the course themes. The theme of risk is the one that we ask you to identify in this topic.

Activity 1.1

Allow 10 minutes

Before you get going on this topic, write down the risks that you feel may be associated with medicinal plants. In so doing, it would be helpful to classify them as naturally occurring (involuntary) and human-induced (voluntary) as set out in the *Introduction to the course*. You should annotate by means of the marginal icon, R, the discussion of risk through the chapters and we will return to your list of risks at the end of the topic (in Activity 5.1).

We will begin with a species of medicinal plant famed throughout the Ancient Greek and Roman Empires.

1.1 The importance of silphion

Silphion (also known as *silphium* or *lasar* in Latin) was a plant used by the Ancient Greeks and Romans for a variety of medicinal purposes, but most famously for birth control. The properties of silphion were widely communicated through the works of contemporary writers and historians. The importance of this plant was indicated by its depiction on artefacts such as coins (Figure 1.1a) and pottery – it may even have had its own Goddess (Figure 1.1b)! Silphion was believed to grow only in and around the city of Cyrene (Figure 1.2a; now in northern Libya) where the plant parts were harvested, processed and then transported around the Mediterranean during the sixth to first centuries BC. A sixth

(a)

(b)

Figure 1.1 (a) Coins depicting the silphion plant, which were minted from 510–375 BC in Cyrene. (b) The Goddess of Silphion (two figures dating from about 300 years BC, from Cyrene, now kept in the Louvre Museum, Paris).

(a)

(b)

Figure 1.2 (a) The ruins of Cyrene.
(b) A sixth century BC cup in the Louvre believed
to depict the weighing and loading of silphion.

century BC cup in the Louvre Museum in Paris is believed to show the King of
Cyrene overseeing the weighing and loading of silphion onto ships (Figure 1.2b).
Pliny the Elder (23–79 AD) wrote that large amounts of public money were used
to import silphion to Rome at the start of the civil war (49 BC). According to Pliny,
the plant was 'very famous for its potency', 'magnificent in general use and in
medicines' and 'among the most exceptional gifts of nature' (Fisher, 1996). The
demand for the plant was such that, about 700 years after it was first known, it
became extinct, probably due to overharvesting. It was reported by Pliny that the
last stalk of silphion was presented to the Emperor Nero in the first century AD. It
is likely that in the latter years of its use, silphion was a highly valuable and
scarce commodity, available only to the wealthy and powerful.

The use of silphion as a contraceptive or as an abortifacient (for abortion in the
early stages of pregnancy) was well established according to both Hippocrates
and Pliny. It was also said by Pliny to 'cleanse retained afterbirth from the
womb', or 'to control the menses [menstruation]' which may have been a
euphemism for birth control. Just as modern medicines require instructions for
use, medicinal plants often came with lengthy directions for preparation and
administering. Silphion could either be taken orally – prepared as a tea from the
leaves – or by soaking a small piece of wool in the plant sap and using it as a
pessary. The biochemical and physiological basis of the action of medicinal plants
similar to silphion is considered in Chapter 4.

It was not unusual for medicinal plants, especially ones with notable therapeutic
uses, such as silphion, to be assigned a variety of other uses, some of which may
be spurious. According to Pliny, silphion could be used to treat leprosy, restore
hair, and serve as an antidote to poison. Unusually for medicinal plants, many of

which have toxic parts or can be harmful if consumed in large amounts, the whole of the silphion plant was known to be edible to humans and livestock. 'In the kitchen, for example, it could be used as a spice to add to a sauce for roast bird or lamb [...] or as a sauce for a ray' (Fisher, 1996). The crop was thought to be very beneficial to sheep, making them healthier, fattening them and improving the flavour of the meat. In fact, consumption of the silphion plant by humans or excessive grazing by livestock may have contributed to its demise. So silphion was not only a plant with wide-ranging medicinal uses but also an important source of food.

Several of the themes of the course emerge in the story of silphion. Communication of the uses and status of silphion, e.g. via coinage or ancient texts, was vital to its success. Birth control and overexploitation of a natural resource would be considered ethical issues today (see later in this chapter), as would the risk to health (see Chapter 4), but did they matter to the Greeks or Romans? There are suggestions that the ethical issues of birth control were in fact debated. The following discussion of ethical issues and the quotations are taken from an article by Fisher (1996).

C E

Pliny expressed hostility to medical assistance for abortion, and gave fewer references to mechanisms for preventing pregnancy than other authors:

> It is notable then that when he discusses the medical uses of lasar (silphion), his first mention concerns the use of the leaves for purging the womb and expelling miscarried fetuses, and the third use of lasar juice mentioned is that it is given in wine to women, or applied (as a pessary) on soft wool, to produce menstruation.

The ethical issues of silphion use are also alluded to in a poem by Catullus (born in 84 BC in Verona), which tells of his love for an older woman, Lesbia:

> You ask, how many kisses of yours are enough, Lesbia, for me and to spare. As great a number as of Libyan sands which lie at lasar-bearing Cyrene between the oracle of sweltering Jove and the sacred sepulchre of ancient Battus.

It was likely that Lesbia was choosing a lifestyle that required contraception. She was portrayed as a married woman (or widow) of the highest wealth and nobility, who had borne children, but who was seeking love and sexual pleasures with a succession of partners:

> The poet would thus by the lasar-allusion be indicating his awareness of what was believed to be an important, if rather secretive, aspect of the lives of such independent women.

Senior Roman figures 'could be expected to be outraged by recourse to birth control [...] as well as scandalised (and amused) by the gossip of adulteries and divorces'. There may also have been some concern about risks to health. For example, Soranus, whose first two suggestions for oral contraceptives or abortifacients are recipes involving 'Cyrenaic juice' (i.e. silphion products), gave warnings of side-effects. We will return to some of these debates of ethical issues and risk in human reproduction in a modern parallel to silphion in Chapter 4.

1.2   The identification of silphion

The illustrations on coins (Figure 1.1a) and written descriptions of silphion are sufficiently comprehensive for us to be able to identify the plant to **family** level. The family is one of the most convenient and widely used means of classifying plants and will be used extensively in this book. The family is a formal level of biological classification above the level of genus and species and below the level of order (Figure 1.3). A family may contain one or more genera (plural of genus) comprising one or more species, whilst an order may contain one or more families. Every species has a two-part scientific name, which starts with the name of the genus. For example, the scientific name of annual meadow grass is *Poa annua* where *Poa* is the genus name. Note the convention that the genus name starts with a capital letter and that the whole scientific name is written in italics. There are many species in the genus *Poa*, which is in the family Poaceae, otherwise known as the grasses. This family contains many genera besides *Poa*, including *Phyllostachys* (a genus of bamboo) and *Saccharum* (species *officinarum*, sugar cane). The order Poales includes the family Poaceae and related families such as the Bromeliaceae (Figure 1.3).

Other plant families include the Asteraceae (the daisy family) and the Orchidaceae (the orchid family), both of which contain many thousands of species. All the members of a family have a set of common characteristics, e.g. seed or flower shape, which distinguish them from other families. Characteristics such as flower parts or pollen structure, which vary little within the study group (e.g. species or family), are more important for classification than highly variable features, such as leaf size or plant height. Classification is not simply a filing convenience. The similarity of species is used to infer ancestral relationships – the greater the similarity of species, the more recent their common ancestor is likely to be. From knowledge of the characteristics of species today, we can hypothesise the most likely evolutionary changes in the past, thereby generating phylogenetic

Figure 1.3   Classification of flowering plants. The diagram shows the hierarchy levels from phylum down to species, using *Poa annua* (annual meadow grass) as an example.

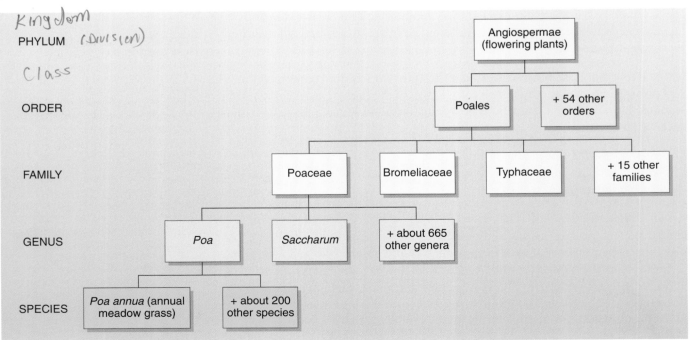

trees which show how species may have evolved from common ancestors over given timescales. Most of this work is now undertaken with molecular data (e.g. comparing base sequences of DNA or amino acid sequences of proteins).

Activity 1.2

Allow 20 minutes throughout topic

You are going to encounter many plant names in this topic. You may find it helpful to draw up a table of the plant names and the uses of the plants. The table should have columns, headed 'Family', 'Scientific name (genus and species)', 'Common name', 'Medicinal use' and 'Related plants'. You should also include a note of the page/section where the plant was mentioned. There are several tables in this book that can be used as sources for your table (e.g. Table 2.1).

■   Look at Figure 1.4, which shows two living plant species and compare these with the images of silphion in Figure 1.1a. What characteristics of silphion are apparent on these ancient coins?

■   The lines depicting grooves on the stems, the overlapping leaf bases, the large terminal flower-head and the secondary flower-heads.

Of course such characteristics may be artistic invention, but it is likely that the original drawings were attempts to illustrate the plant as accurately as possible. These characteristics place silphion in the family **Apiaceae** (formerly known as the Umbelliferae – both names are given here, as many texts still use the old name). The Apiaceae contain many familiar culinary species, including carrot, parsley, parsnip, celery, coriander and fennel (Figure 1.4a). The flowering parts of a plant are particularly important for describing the species. You will see in

C

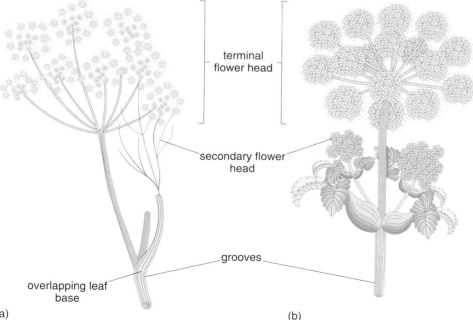

(a)   (b)

Figure 1.4   Examples of species in the plant family Apiaceae. (a) Fennel (*Foeniculum vulgare*). (b) Alexanders (*Smyrnium olusatrum*), a plant with leaves that taste similar to celery. Note the similarities to the images on the coins in Figure 1.1a.

Figure 1.4 that Apiaceae have very characteristic flower-heads (umbels). The fruit is also characteristic, comprising two (often flattened) seed capsules, as seen in some coins depicting silphion. Thus, although silphion is extinct, it is possible to determine its close relatives alive today.

Some of the earliest references to medicinal plants are to silphion and other members of the Apiaceae; for example, coriander was first mentioned in a very early Greek script called *Linear B* (about 1000 BC). Besides species with culinary or medicinal uses, the Apiaceae has many species that are highly poisonous, including hemlock (*Conium maculatum*), which Socrates was required to drink after being condemned to death. We will see later that it is not unusual for members of the same plant family to be of both benefit and harm to humans.

1.3 Overharvesting of medicinal plants

E

We have no information on whether the overharvesting of silphion was a concern at the time or whether any lessons were learnt from the loss of silphion. However, the large trade in plants for medicines is a concern today, especially with the renewed interest in traditional medicines. This is made explicit in an article from *New Scientist*, 10 January 2004, entitled 'No remedy in sight for herbal ransack' (Extract 1.1).

Activity 1.3

Allow 45 minutes

Read Extract 1.1, then write an brief description of the key ethical issue in the extract.

Extract 1.1 No remedy in sight for herbal ransack

By Rob Edwards

Natural remedies are so popular that many wild plants are being harvested to the point of extinction

THE multimillion-pound boom in herbal medicine is threatening to wipe out up to a fifth of the plant species on which it depends, wrecking their natural habitats and jeopardising the health of millions of people in developing countries. And yet the herbal medicines industry has been accused of doing nothing about it.

Most people around the globe use herbal medicine for everyday healthcare, with as many as 80 per cent relying on it in some countries. But two-thirds of the 50 000 medicinal plants in use are still harvested from the wild, and research to be published later this year suggests that between 4000 and 10 000 of them may now be endangered.

A study by Alan Hamilton, a plant specialist from the global environment network WWF, will point out that the market for herbal remedies in North

America and Europe has been expanding by about 10 per cent a year for the last decade and the world market is now thought to be worth at least £11 billion. Many of the plants are harvested by poor communities in India and China whose livelihoods will suffer if the plants die out.

'It's an extremely serious problem', Hamilton told *New Scientist*. He is a member of the World Conservation Union's Medicinal Plants Specialist Group, and has drawn his estimates of the number of species at risk from expert analyses of the IUCN's Red List of threatened plants. His study is due to be published in *Biodiversity and Conservation*.

Hamilton has also helped compile a report, *Herbal Harvests with a Future*, which is due to be unveiled next week by the conservation group Plantlife International. 'With demand and commercialisation growing fast, the future of the wild plants which have helped most of humanity for centuries is now more uncertain than it has ever been', says the group's Martin Harper.

One species highlighted by Plantlife as being under threat is tetu lakha (*Nothatodytes foetida*), a small tree found in rainforests in south India and Sri Lanka and used for anti-cancer drugs in Europe. Others include a saw-wort known as costus or kusta (*Saussurea lappa*) from India whose root is used for chronic skin disorders, and the tendrilled fritillary (*Fritillaria cirrhosa*) from Sichuan, China, used to treat respiratory infections.

Although the crisis has been looming for years, Plantlife accuses the herbal medicine industry of failing to ensure the sustainability of its supplies. It has established that 11 of 16 herbal companies in the UK, for instance, harvest all the plants they sell from the wild, and the remaining five grow only a small proportion.

A leading UK natural skin care company, The Body Shop International, accepts that it doesn't grow its own medicinal plants, but insists that it is environmentally aware. 'The protection of flora and fauna is an integral part of The Body Shop approach to products. We do not source materials derived from endangered and threatened species', says a company spokeswoman in London.

But Plantlife says awareness of the environmental problems among companies in general is limited and sometimes vague. 'Given the scale of the threat, this is alarming', Harper warns. 'It is time for the industry to join forces with environmental organisations to ensure that herbal harvests have a sustainable future'.

Another leading international expert on medicinal plants, Gerard Bodeker from Green College, Oxford, thinks that the assessments of the crisis by Hamilton and Plantlife are conservative. Most of the processes involved in supplying the growing market for herbal remedies are 'the result of unsustainable and often destructive practices driven by poverty', he says. The industry is characterised by changing health fads which keep favouring different plants, so there is little incentive to sustainably produce particular species, he argues. 'They are eating their own nest. They are not replacing what they take'.

The market for African cherry (*Prunus africana*), the bark of which is popular in Europe as a treatment for prostate enlargement, has collapsed because too many trees have been destroyed. In the past the trees, which grow in Africa's mountain regions, survived because traditionally less than half of their bark was harvested.

But according to a recent study by Kristine Stewart, from consultants Keith and Schnars in Florida, growing commercial pressures have led to whole forests being stripped or felled. Exports of dried bark halved between 1997 and 2000 and the main exporter, Plantecam, had to close its extraction factory in Cameroon (*Journal of Ethnopharmacology*, vol. **89**, p. 3).

In its report, Plantlife urges the industry to invest in cultivation. It also proposes the introduction of a kite mark to identify products that have been sustainably harvested. 'There is a complete lack of awareness and lack of education amongst consumers', Bodeker says. Although those that use herbal medicines might be expected to be more environmentally aware than most, that doesn't seem to be the case. 'They don't make the links', he adds. The UK's largest association of herbal practitioners, the National Institute of Medical Herbalists, is very concerned. 'We all need to work together to address this issue and to put pressure on suppliers', the institute's Trudy Norris says. 'The future of the wild plants which have helped most of humanity for centuries is now more uncertain than ever.'

Whilst over-exploitation is a genuine concern, efforts are also being made to undertake **sustainable harvesting** of plant populations for medicinal use, i.e. to ensure that the future survival of the plant is not compromised by current levels of use and harvesting practice. An example of a plant species that is currently subject to sustainable harvesting is ground hemlock (*Taxus canadensis*, Figure 1.5), which is found mainly on the eastern coast of Canada. Notice that this hemlock is *not* related to the hemlock in the Apiaceae (above).

Figure 1.5   Ground hemlock (*Taxus canadensis*).

Plants in the genus *Taxus* (yews) have a long history of use in traditional medicine. *Taxus canadensis* was employed medicinally by several native North American Indian tribes who used small amounts of the leaves both internally and externally to treat rheumatism, fevers, influenza and to expel afterbirth (like silphion; in fact, various *Taxus* species have been used to control the female reproductive system – see Chapter 4). Compounds in the shoots and bark, collectively known as taxanes, have been studied and a taxane derivative called **taxol** (Figure 1.6) was developed as an important anti-cancer drug, particularly in the treatment of ovarian cancer. Taxol was originally isolated from the Pacific yew (*Taxus brevifolia*) and is sourced from European yew (*Taxus baccata*) in addition to *Taxus canadensis*. We will discuss the structure and function of medicinally active plant compounds and their use in drug development in Chapters 3–5.

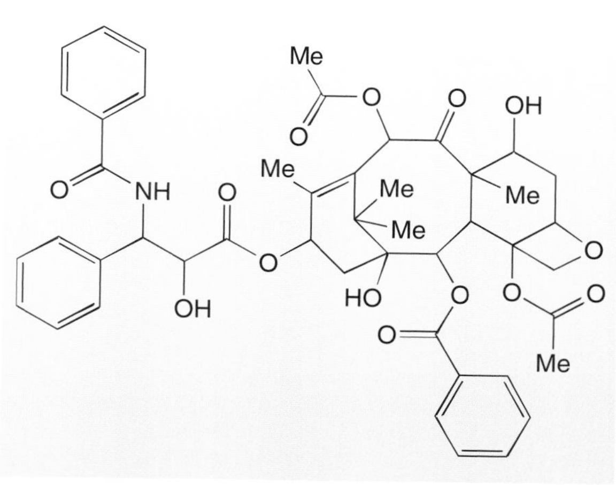

Figure 1.6   Structure of the anti-cancer drug taxol. (Me = methyl group, $-CH_3$.)

You will see that many of the medicinally active molecules discussed in this topic have complex chemical structures, some of which are shown either in the main text or in the Appendix. It is not necessary for you to understand the details of these chemical structures. Rather, your aim should be to appreciate, in general terms, the similarity or otherwise between one structure and another.

In the first 10 years of commercial harvesting of yew species from the wild, uncontrolled and unregulated exploitation produced deleterious effects on several species. This was a particular concern in Canada. In response, the Canadian Forestry Service (in 2002) set levels and protocols for harvesting of *Taxus canadensis*. These recommendations include minimum size of plants for harvesting and the cutting of selected shoots with hand pruners. Harvesting levels are set at approximately 2 million kg of plant biomass per year, which yields approximately 80 kg of taxanes. These harvesting levels are best maintained within managed areas, where 400 kg of plant biomass may be sustainably harvested from 1 ha, with harvests every four years.

■ What is the annual rate of sustainable harvesting of plant biomass per hectare?

   400 kg ha^{-1} every four years = 100 kg ha^{-1} y^{-1}.

■ How many km^2 are required to meet the target of 80 kg of taxanes per year?

   The amount of plant biomass required to yield 80 kg of taxane per year is 2 million kg. So the number of hectares that have to be harvested per year is

$$\frac{2\,000\,000\,\text{kg}}{100\,\text{kg}\,\text{ha}^{-1}} = 20\,000\,\text{ha} \quad \text{or } 2 \times 10^4 \text{ ha}$$

1 ha = 100 m × 100 m = 10^4 m^2

so 2×10^4 ha = 2×10^8 m^2 = 200×10^6 m^2 = 200 km^2

(which is approximately equal to an area of 14 km × 14 km).

1.4 Silphion as a brand name

C

Although silphion is extinct, its name lives on, serving as a reminder of the importance of conservation, an attribute it shares with another extinct species, the dodo. The Medicinal Plant Specialist group of IUCN (International Union for Conservation of Nature and Natural Resources) has an image of silphion as its logo (Figure 1.7a). Silphion also persists as a brand name for healthcare products, suggesting its name is a potent symbol of a cure-all. An example is given here of a silphion 'tonic' (a combination of fruits and herbs, Figure 1.7b), although the use of this product has nothing in common with the original primary use of silphion!

Figure 1.7   Rebranding of silphion. (a) The IUCN logo. (b) Silphion tonic, one of several dozen dietary supplements produced and marketed by the German company Naka Herbs & Vitamins.

(a)

(b)

Summary of Chapter 1

Silphion was a plant exploited in the Greek and Roman periods for its medicinal properties, especially in birth control. The plant became extinct in the first century AD but its depiction on coins and other artefacts allows it to be placed in the plant family Apiaceae.

Silphion was probably lost due to overharvesting, a fate that may befall other medicinal plants in use today. Sustainable harvesting practices, as illustrated with ground hemlock, need to be put in place to ensure future generations of humans can benefit from the global wealth of medicinal plants (such as the anti-cancer drug taxol).

The silphion brand is potent both as a powerful medicine and an example of an extinct species.

The source and consolidation of medicinal plant knowledge

2.1 The origins of medicinal plant knowledge

That silphion and its properties were known over 2500 years ago is a reminder that local rural communities across the planet have been exploring their natural environment over thousands of years, resulting in a huge number and variety of plants with medicinal properties being discovered. We will discuss a selection of these plants in this topic to illustrate different course themes and medicinal applications (see Table 2.1; some of the drugs developed from these products and their global usage are discussed in Chapters 4 and 5).

Table 2.1 Sources of some medicinal plant products.

Medicinal product	Plant species	Region of origin	Original users of plant	Where discussed in this topic
Muscle relaxant in surgery	curare vine (*Curarea* species)	Ecuador	South American Indians	Chapters 2 and 5
Anti-cancer agent	rosy periwinkle (*Catharanthus roseus*)	Madagascar		Chapters 3 and 5
Anti-cancer agent	ground hemlock (*Taxus canadensis*)	Eastern Canada	North American Indians	Chapter 1
Pain relief, possible hormonal regulation	wild yam (*Dioscorea villosa*)	South and Central America	Mayans, Aztecs	Chapter 4
Anti-malarial treatment	wormwood (*Artemisia* species)	China		Chapter 5
Possible anti-depressant	St John's wort (*Hypericum perforatum*)	Europe	Western Europeans	Chapters 2 and 4

How was knowledge of the medicinal effects of plants first gained? How did the properties of plants such as silphion first come to attention? Chance must have played a role in the origins of much early plant knowledge. Individuals happened to notice a new plant and possibly tasted or consumed it. They may have felt better (or worse!) after doing so and attributed those feelings of health, or otherwise, to consumption of the plant. It is also likely that there was some more systematic observation and testing involved. One possibility is that people observed the effects of plants on other animals, perhaps on animals similar to themselves, such as other primates. There are records of gorillas and chimpanzees eating hallucinogenic plants and undergoing frenzied behaviour, as though they were being chased. Observation of effects on livestock may also have been important, perhaps in the case of silphion. Once humans decided to try a leaf or chew a piece of bark, the taste would also be important. Plants containing medicinally useful compounds often have a bitter taste (for reasons that will become clear later). A combination of information, such as avoidance or consumption by herbivores, taste and smell, may have persuaded people to experiment with some crude extracts of all or part of the plant, e.g. incorporating the products into a bush tea (the combination of water and heat allowing the release of the active ingredients). Indeed, early use of medicinal plants would have had much in common with early trials of food plants. Both of these activities required a close knowledge of the natural environment and suggest applications of scientific method.

C

Observations of the potential medicinal worth of plants in Europe were also subject to divine guidance. It was believed, under the **Doctrine of Signatures**, that the Creator would direct humans to the medicinal uses of a particular plant. Thus, a plant good for the lungs would have a part with a shape reminiscent of a lung (the similarity may be loose!). Medicinally useful plants were also believed to thrive in places where the diseases occurred. This philosophy was particularly important in the 17th century, being closely linked with astrology and promoted by leading herbalists such as Nicholas Culpeper (1616–1654). The doctrine focused people's attention on detailed characteristics of the plants. This knowledge often became embedded in the common name of the plant, e.g. lungwort, where 'wort' comes from Old English 'wyrt', which meant herb or plant, especially with a medicinal use. Many examples of such common names have survived today, including milkwort, birthwort and lousewort, along with other common names that suggest medical uses, such as fleabane and eyebright. Some of the later scientific names (genus and species) also drew on these early references to medical use, e.g. lungwort is in the genus *Pulmonaria*, from the Latin *pulmo* (lung).

(a)

(b)

Figure 2.1 St John's wort (*Hypercium perforatum*). (a) Flowers. (b) Leaves; note the translucent spots resembling holes in the leaf.

One particularly interesting case of a 'wort' species is **St John's wort** (Figure 2.1). This common name is applied to various species in the genus *Hypericum*, the name of which is probably derived from 'hyper' and 'eikon' meaning 'over' and 'image' (icon), referring to it being placed over sacred objects to help ward off evil. Indeed, St John's wort is surrounded by a rich pagan and Christian folklore deduced from the plant's structure and timing of flowering. St John's wort was given its common name because it flowered on the feast day of St John the Baptist (24 June). The description in Gerard's 17th century herbal (discussed later in this chapter) suggests that the plant works on deep wounds and those that are through the body. This association comes from the translucent spots on the leaves which, when held up to the light, look like holes (cover picture and Figure 2.1b). These are a good characteristic for identifying certain *Hypericum* species and noted by Gerard in the early 17th century:

> many small and narrow leaves, which if you behold betwixt your eies and the light, do appeare as it were bored or thrust thorow in an infinite number of places with pinnes pointes.

The red sap of some species led to the belief that the spots in the leaves ooze blood on 29 August, the day of St John's execution. The arrangements of stamens (male flower parts, Figure 2.1a) on the flower reminded people of the crown of thorns worn by Jesus, so the plant was used to relieve headaches. St John's wort was also associated with the devil, driving out the inner devil and keeping Satan at bay. The old associations of medicinal use of St John's wort for the head and the inner devil are reflected in its modern use as a medicine for treating depression, discussed in Chapter 4.

C

In many cultures, the early communication of knowledge about medicinal properties of plants was based on an **oral communication**, with the knowledge often held by one or two key members of a community and only passed on to selected individuals. Such oral traditions are still in evidence in indigenous peoples in parts of the world such as Amazonia and Borneo. Knowledge restricted to the minds of a few individuals is unsafe, as the information could die with its owner or the information could change as it passed down through generations. As languages have been lost and traditional cultures replaced by globally homogeneous views, so much of the medicinal plant knowledge base has disappeared. It is ironic that the consolidation of information in written form, which has often required the intrusion of Europeans, is now the only way that many indigenous groups can learn about their former culture. The following example of the arrow poison, curare, illustrates this point.

2.2 The transfer of knowledge of curare from Amerindians to Europeans

The original inhabitants of South America (Amerindians) were the first people to discover and develop **curare** as an arrow poison and recognise some of its beneficial medicinal properties, e.g. in combating diarrhoea. Once Europeans knew of curare's existence and some of its properties, they became desperate to determine its composition and carry that knowledge to their own countries. Explorations by Europeans in the area now covered by Guyana (Figure 2.2) in the late 18th to mid-19th century led to dissemination of the Amerindian knowledge of curare.

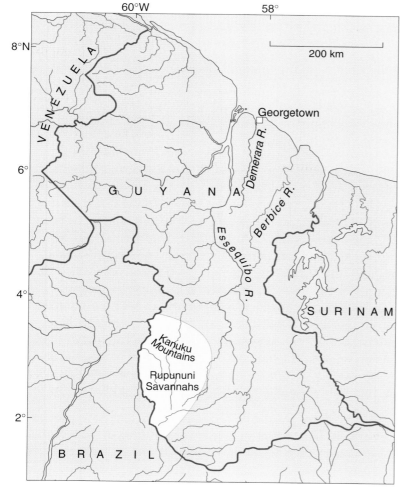

Figure 2.2   Map of Guyana and northeast South America, showing the major rivers.

Edward Bancroft was one of the first to report on curare from present-day Guyana. His account in 1769 considered the use and preparation of curare by the Akawai living near the sources of the Essequibo, Demerara and Berbice rivers (Figure 2.2). Bancroft noted that:

> these arrows are used in hunting, but particularly for killing monkeys […] when pricked with a poison arrow their limbs become useless, and they fall to the ground. But I do not find, that even in their wars, which are seldom, they ever attack any of the human species with poisoned arrows.

C

Charles Waterton (Figure 2.3) travelled extensively in Guyana, recording the details of his travels and spreading the news of curare to a wider audience. Waterton's *Wanderings in South America* became one of the most reprinted books of the 19th century and hence an important lesson in the communication of knowledge. The Waterton family owned a plantation house, Walton Hall, on the Atlantic coast of Guyana. This house shared the name of the ancestral home near Wakefield in Yorkshire, England (and, by coincidence, the name of the home of the Open University in Milton Keynes!). The extracts quoted below are from the 1825 edition of Waterton's book, which bore the unwieldy title of *Wanderings in South America, the North-west of the United States and the Antilles in the years 1812, 1816, 1820, with original instructions for the perfect preservation of birds etc. for cabinets of natural history*.

In April 1812 Waterton set out from Stabroek (as the capital Georgetown, shown on Figure 2.2, was then known) on his first journey, with the clear objective 'to collect a quantity of the strongest wourali poison'. Wourali was the name by which Waterton knew curare. Although Waterton frequently interspersed his account of the journey with poetic tales of the wildlife and people he met, he also provided detailed and accurate descriptions of everyday life, e.g. the consumption of cassava bread and boiled fish, which remain the staples of many Amerindian people today. It was at one of the Amerindian settlements that Waterton obtained a 'small quantity of the wourali poison'.

> It was in a little gourd. The Indian who had it, said that he had killed a number of wild hogs with it, and two tapirs […] Its strength was proved on a middle-sized dog. He was wounded in the thigh, in order that there might be no possibility of touching a vital part. In three or four minutes he began to be affected, smelt at every little thing on the ground around him, and looked wistfully at the wounded part. Soon after this he staggered, laid himself down, and never rose more. He now put his head betwixt his fore legs, and raising it slowly again, he fell over on his side. His eye immediately became fixed, and though his extremities every now and then shot convulsively, he never showed the least desire to raise up his head. His heart fluttered much from the time he laid down, and at intervals beat very strong; then stopped for a moment or two; and then beat again, and continued faintly beating several minutes, after every other part of his body seemed dead. In a quarter of an hour after he had received the poison he was quite motionless.

E

This account is remarkable in its focus on detailed observation of the behavioural and physiological response of the dog to the curare. Of course, such an

Figure 2.3   A portrait of Charles Waterton (1782–1865).

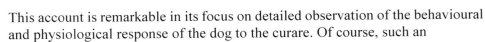

experiment today would raise serious ethical issues. This study reflected Waterton's interest in testing the poison (he tried it out on a donkey following his return to England – see Chapter 5). Waterton was also fascinated by the rich variety of the plant life around him and its potential uses:

> No doubt, there is many a balsam and many a medicinal root yet to be discovered, and many a resin, gum, and oil yet unnoticed.

Finally, in the southwest of Guyana near the Brazilian border, he entered a new region:

> You are now within the borders of Macoushia, inhabited by a different tribe of people, called Macoushi Indians; uncommonly dextrous in the use of the blowpipe, and famous for their skill in preparing the deadly vegetable poison, commonly called Wourali.

This area of Guyana is in the Rupununi Savannah (Figure 2.2), where the Macushi still live today. The Macushi were reputed to have the most effective form of curare. It was believed that their poison would take a few minutes to work, while that made on the Rio Negro or Orinoco may take hours. At this point in the text, Waterton emphasises the importance of wourali to one of the communities in the region.

> The Indians […] seemed to depend more on the wourali poison for killing their game, than upon anything else. They had only one gun, and it appeared rusty and neglected; but their poisoned weapons were in fine order. Their blow-pipes hung from the roof of the hut, carefully suspended by a silk grass cord; and on taking a nearer view of them, no dust seemed to have collected there, nor had the spider spun the smallest web on them; which showed that they were in constant use. The quivers were close by them, with the jaw-bone of the fish Perai [piranha] tied by a string to their brim, and a small wicker basket of wild cotton, which hung down to their centre: they were nearly full of poisoned arrows. It was with difficulty these Indians could be persuaded to part with any of the wourali poison, though a good price was offered for it: they gave to understand that it was powder and shot to them and very difficult to be procured.

Despite Waterton's interest and enthusiasm, he failed to get an account of how the poison was made, although he did succeed in bringing some of it back to England. The final information on the composition of the Macushi curare had to wait for the investigations of the Schomburgk brothers.

Robert Schomburgk (Figure 2.4) was born in Freiburg, Prussia but worked for most of his life for Britain and its overseas territories and was knighted for his services. He established the boundary of British Guiana with Venezuela, called the Schomburgk Line. Robert first visited Guyana in 1835–36 and was later (in 1840) accompanied by his younger brother Richard (1811–1890).

Robert Schomburgk made three attempts to discover the plant(s) with which the Macushi made curare and to observe its manufacture. He knew that the most important plant, and the name given to the local form of the arrow poison, was **urari** (probably equivalent to Waterton's wourali). In 1835–36, in the company

Figure 2.4 Robert Schomburgk (1804–1865).

of a Wapishiana (an Amerindian group living alongside the Macushi) who knew how to make the poison, he visited the Kanuku Mountains to find the urari vine. This specimen only had fruit, so he could not give a full botanical description. However, he did recognise it as a new species of *Strychnos* which he named **Strychnos toxifera** (Figure 2.5). The specimen is in the herbarium of the Royal Botanic Gardens at Kew. In 1837 he again failed to collect flowering specimens. On this occasion he was accompanied by a Macushi curare maker.

Figure 2.5   *Strychnos toxifera* growing in Guyana.

■   Why was it important for Robert Schomburgk to find a *Strychnos toxifera* specimen in flower?

▨   Floral characteristics are important for determining the relationship of the specimen to other known species, i.e. in classifying the plant in a genus or family (Chapter 1). Later such characteristics would have been used to infer evolutionary relationships.

He then asked the Reverend Youd, living at Pirara on the Rupununi, to see if he could persuade any curare makers to show him the preparation. This was achieved, and in October 1838 Youd sent a letter to Schomburgk giving an account of the composition:

urari, bark (*Strychnos toxifera*)	2 lb
arimaru, bark (*Strychnos cogens*)	¼ lb
tarireng (unidentified)	¼ lb
yakki (*Strychnos bredemeyeri*)	¼ lb
wakarimo (unidentified)	¼ lb
tararemu, from the root of the tarireng vine	½ oz
muramu (*Cissus* species), bulbous root soaked in the half-cooked poison and the mucilage squeezed from it to thicken the poison	1¼ lb
manacu, very bitter bark of a large tree (*Zanthoxylum* species)	4 small pieces

Robert Schomburgk finally saw curare being prepared in Pirara in 1839. The flowering *Strychnos toxifera* were found by his brother Richard. Whilst urari was the most important ingredient, some of the other ingredients listed above may have helped increase the toxicity, bind the mixture to the arrow or increase the uptake of the poison. Two of the other ingredients (arimaru and yakki) were different *Strychnos* species. There were also more fanciful ingredients such as snake teeth (not listed above). By about the 1930s, the Macushi had lost the knowledge of how to make urari – without Robert Schomburgk, that knowledge would have been lost altogether.

An important contribution to the communication of plant knowledge was the use of scientific names rather than the local names.

■ Why is the use of scientific names important for communication?   *C*

▨ Because each species has one unique name, whereas a species may have several different or no common names; alternatively, the same common name may apply to different species. For example, recall that the name hemlock is given to two unrelated species (*Taxus canadensis* and *Conium maculatum*).

The need for a scientific name is highlighted by the fact that there were about eight Amerindian languages in existence in Guyana, several of which had names for curare components. However, the only *Strychnos* known as urari in Akawai and orari in Arawak was *Strychnos toxifera*. In Creole, *Strychnos toxifera* is curare; all other *Strychnos* species in Creole are devildoer. Thus *Strychnos toxifera* is recognised in all three languages as important and different from the other *Strychnos* vines.

You may ask why this account of an arrow poison is relevant to medicinal plants. Surprisingly, it is possible that you have benefited from curare! This is because curare extracts were used as muscle relaxants in surgery in the mid-20th century and provided the basis for the development of compounds that are now used routinely in operations. We will discuss the use of curare as a muscle relaxant in Chapter 3 and the way in which drugs were developed from it in Chapter 5.

2.3 The dissemination and formalisation of knowledge in herbals

The example of curare demonstrates how written communication can consolidate   *C*
medicinal plant knowledge, ensuring that the key constituents are accurately described.

■ What are the important distinctions between oral and written communication?

▨ In the former case, knowledge is passed from one person to a relatively small audience and the knowledge may be lost or modified with time. In the latter case, knowledge can be disseminated to many people over many years, often with the original words available for scrutiny.

The dual function of dissemination to a wide audience over long timescales and accurate description is exemplified in the great tradition of **herbals**, which were books describing the characteristics and uses of medicinal plants, starting with the Greeks over 2000 years ago. The most important of the Greek herbalists was

Dioscorides (Figure 2.6a), born in the first century AD in southeast Asia Minor (Tarsus, now in Turkey). His work *De Materia Medica* ('On Medical Matters', written about 50–70 AD) contained descriptions of about 600 plants and 1000 medicines derived from those plants (Figure 2.6b). The earliest surviving copy is from the fifth century AD (the work was preserved exclusively by Arabic people until the 10th century).

Figure 2.6 (a) The Greek herbalist Dioscorides. (b) A plate from *De Materia Medica*.

(b)

(a)

Theophrastus, a pupil of Aristotle writing in the fourth century BC, and Pliny the Elder (Chapter 1), a Roman contemporary of Dioscorides, also made important contributions to the wider knowledge of plants. Theophrastus was one of the first to show any insights into ecology. The translation of *De Materia Medica* in the 15th century reflected a new wave of interest in plant medicines in Europe, continuing through to the British herbalists such as John Gerard in the 16th and 17th centuries (Figure 2.7a) and Nicholas Culpeper in the 17th century.

Figure 2.7 (a) John Gerard (1564–1637). (b) Frontispiece from the 1636 edition of Gerard's *The Herball or Generall Historie of Plantes*.

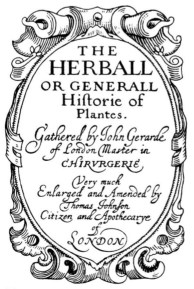

(a)

(b)

The herbals were an important bridge between orally communicated knowledge and modern electronic databases of plant knowledge. They embraced the requirement for accurate description and contributed to the move from common to scientific names. We will discuss these ideas in relation to the herbal of John Gerard and the medicinally important plants with the common name of **henbane**. In so doing, we will illustrate the transition from folklore to systematic study, opening the way for the development of a wide variety of pharmaceutical products.

2.3.1 Henbane

John Gerard was born in 1564 in Nantwich, Cheshire. The first edition of his herbal, entitled *Generall Historie of Plantes*, was published in 1597, but it is the enlarged and amended edition by Thomas Johnson in 1636 that is generally known (Figure 2.7b). Gerard described three species of henbane, so called because it was observed that hens that ate the seeds became ill. A number of characteristics (Table 2.2) and diagrams (e.g. Figure 2.8) were provided to help identify the plants, and can still be used to accurately determine their identity. The phrases used in Tables 2.2 and 2.3 are taken directly from an edited early 20th century edition of Gerard's herbal which retained the wording of the 1636 edition.

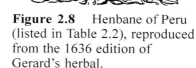

Figure 2.8   Henbane of Peru (listed in Table 2.2), reproduced from the 1636 edition of Gerard's herbal.

Table 2.2   Characteristics of three types of henbane according to Gerard 1636.

Type of plant	Overall size, stem and leaves	Flowers	Fruits/seeds	Locations	Flowering time
henbane	Great, soft stalkes. Leaves very broad, soft, woolly, somewhat jagged.	Bell-fashion, feint yellowish-white and brown within towards the bottom.	Hard knobby husks like small cups or boxes, wherein are brown seeds.	Everywhere by highways, in the borders of fields about dunghills and untilled places.	August [...] seed ripe in October.
yellow henbane	Height of two cubits*. Stalke is thicke, fat and green. Smooth and even leaves, thick and full of juice.	Grows at the tops of branches, orderly placed, of a pale yellow colour.		Sowne in gardens, where it doth prosper exceedingly.	Summer months, [by] Autumne be farre spent.
henbane of Peru	Very great stalkes of bignesse of a childes arme. 7–8 feet high, very faire long leaves, broad, smooth and sharpe pointed.	Floures grow at the top of the stalks, in shape like a bell-floure, somewhat long and cornered, hollow within, of a light carnation colour, tending to whitenesse toward the brims.	Contained in long sharpe pointed seed-vessels.	Growing in fertile and well dunged ground.	[Gerard discusses sowing time but not flowering.]

* A cubit was equal to the length of a forearm.

C

The organisation of the descriptions in Table 2.2 reflects later plant (and animal) studies emphasising the importance of systematically describing all parts, including microscopic features such as pollen. Accurate descriptions are necessary both for identification of other individuals of that species and for determining relationships between species.

■ Recall from Chapter 1 the main levels of classifications for grouping related plant species.

▨ Plant species are grouped successively into genera (singular, genus), families, orders and phyla (Figure 1.3).

In addition to the description of the plants, Gerard also gives the various names by which they are known and the medicinal and other values or uses ('vertues') of the plants (Table 2.3). The relief of pain was an important part of the medical arsenal of two of the species (and possibly also for yellow henbane).

Table 2.3 'Vertues' of the three types of henbane described in Gerard's herbal (see Table 2.2).

Type of henbane	'Vertues'
henbane	Causeth drowsinesse, and mitigateth all kinde of paine
	The root boiled with vinegre, and the same holden hot in the mouth, easeth the pain of the teeth.
yellow henbane	Cure all cuts or hurts in the head
	Doth stupefie or dull the senses, and cause three kind of giddiness that [henbane of Peru] doth.
henbane of Peru	Remedie for the paine of head called the Megram or Migram
	Mitigateth the paine of the gout
	A remedy for the tooth-ache
	Good against poison
	Notable medicines are made hereof against the old and inveterate cough.

C E

Gerard's herbal cuts across two of the themes of the course. The most obvious is *communication*; from the collecting, sifting and reporting of plant form and usage based on a wide variety of oral and written sources, to delivery to an extensive audience over more than 350 years (including, indirectly, students on this course). Gerard also discusses various *ethical* issues associated with plant use. For example, he notes how unscrupulous self-styled medical professionals may prey on individuals in pain or physical distress:

The seed [of henbane] is used by […] tooth-drawers which run about the country, to cause worms come forth of the teeth […] but some crafty companions to gain money convey small lute-strings into the water, persuading the patient that those small creepers came out of his mouth or other parts which he intended to ease.

We will now test whether the descriptions given by Gerard can be used to identify the plants today. This activity is helped by the fact that common names have been retained over many years and sometimes incorporated into modern scientific names by Linnaeus and others (although this can lead to errors, as we will see below). Today henbane is the common name for the species *Hyoscyamus niger*. Indeed Gerard sometimes refers to it as black henbane. The specific name *niger* and common name 'black' do not refer to the colour of the plant but to a belief that parts of the body to which the plant was applied would turn black. Reference to the medicinal and other properties of the plant may be given in modern (popular) floras. For example, in Blamey and Grey-Wilson's *The Illustrated Flora of Britain and Northern Europe* (1989), under *Hyoscyamus niger* they state: 'all parts are poisonous […] its narcotic properties were used to alleviate toothache'. So is this henbane the same as the henbane described by Gerard? Let us consider the characteristics of the modern henbane, *Hyoscyamus niger* (Table 2.4 and Figure 2.9).

■ Do the characteristics of the modern henbane (Table 2.4) agree with those in Gerard's description of henbane (first row in Table 2.2)?

▪ There is a reasonable amount of agreement. This includes:

- leaf shape ('jagged', Gerard; 'coarsely toothed or lobed', Blamey and Grey-Wilson, hereafter B&G-W)
- flower colour ('feint yellowish-white', Gerard; 'pale yellow', B&G-W)
- flower shape ('bell-fashion', Gerard; 'trumpet-shaped', B&G-W)
- fruit shape ('small cups or boxes', Gerard; see Figure 2.9 for B&G-W)
- locations (both agree on bare and disturbed ground and nutrient-rich/dunghills).

Although this is not complete evidence that it is the same species (we would have to check all similar species), it is likely that Gerard was referring to *Hyoscyamus niger*. The other point that emerges from this comparison is that Gerard often gave as much information on plant form as is given in a modern popular text. Floras aimed at professionals will give much more detail including information such as distribution in the UK or Europe. The entry for *Hyoscyamus niger* in the *Excursion Flora of the British Isles* (for many years the simplified

(a)

(b)

Figure 2.9   *Hyoscyamus niger*, (modern) henbane.
(a) Plant in flower. (b) Fruit.

Table 2.4   Characteristics of (modern) henbane, *Hyoscyamus niger*.

Species	Overall size, stem and leaves	Flowers	Fruits/seeds	Locations	Flowering time
henbane (*Hyoscyamus niger*)	Medium to tall, stickily hairy, erect branched to unbranched. Leaves oval to oblong, coarsely toothed or lobed.	Pale yellow, netted with purple veins; irregular trumpet-shaped.	Fruit is a capsule (see Figure 2.9).	Bare and disturbed ground, especially by the sea, on light and nutrient-rich soils.	May to September

students' guide that accompanied the standard text on the British flora by the same authors, reads:

> Annual or biennial up to 80 cm. Hairs soft, glandular. Stem stout. Leaves up to 15–20 cm, with few large teeth or nearly entire, lower stalked, upper sessile and amplexicaul. Flowers *c.* 2 cm, in 2 rows, bracts leaf-like. Corolla 2–3 cm diameter, lurid yellow usually veined with purple. Calyx-tube in fruit 15–20 mm diameter, strongly veined. Flowers June–August. On light soils, especially near the sea, and in farmyards, etc.
>
> (Clapham *et al.*, 1981)

(The text has been amended slightly to expand abbreviations.)

This description, along with scientific names, illustrates the burgeoning technical vocabulary associated with the developing science of (plant) taxonomy. Gerard described plants and their parts in language that could be understood by anybody (who could read!). Thus henbane flowers are bell-shaped and the leaves soft and woolly. Whilst the popular floras may use everyday language, to delve into the scientific literature requires a working knowledge of terms such as calyx, stamen and amplexicaul. (The calyx is the set of green petal-like structures, called sepals, outside the petals; the stamens are the male reproductive structures; and amplexicaul means the leaves clasp the stem.) The breadth of the vocabulary partly reflects the range of variation in structures (e.g. there are many terms to describe the shape of leaves), the number of species and the complexity of their (evolutionary) relationships. Whilst it is a vocabulary borne out of necessity, it is also a vocabulary that excludes those without appropriate training, i.e. it is jargon.

Now we will turn our attention to henbane of Peru. This turns out to be a very familiar plant – it is the tobacco plant, *Nicotiana tabacum* (Table 2.5; Gerard uses similar names, see Table 2.6), which is derived, like curare, from South America.

Table 2.5 Characteristics of the tobacco plant, *Nicotiana tabacum*.

Species	Overall size; stem and leaves	Flowers	Fruits/seeds	Locations	Flowering time
Tobacco (*Nicotiana tabacum*)	Tall, stickily-hairy, strong smelling, up to 2 m tall and more. Leaves large and elliptical to lanceolate (long, narrow, gradually tapering) and toothed.	Pale green or creamish, often with pink tinge; trumpet-shaped.	Green capsule	Cultivated land, waste places; especially on arable land.	June to August

Table 2.6 Names given to the three types of 'henbane' by Gerard and the current scientific names. Note that only *Hyoscyamus niger* is native to Britain.

Gerard name	Other names given by Gerard	Modern scientific names
Henbane	Common blacke Henbane	*Hyoscyamus niger*
Yellow Henbane, or English Tabaco	Hyoscyamus luteus, Nicotiana (of Nicot, a Frenchman who brought seeds from the Indies); Dubius Hyoscyamus, or doubtfull Henbane	*Nicotiana rusticana* (probably)
Henbane of Peru	Petun, Sacra herba, Sancta herba, Sanasancta indorum, Hyoscyamus Peruvianus, Tabacum, Tabaco	*Nicotiana tabacum*

■   What are the main similarities and differences between this description of *Nicotiana tabacum* and Gerard's 'henbane of Peru'?

▪   Both are of similar height. It is not clear if the leaves are the same. Flower shape appears to be similar (bell- and trumpet-shaped), as does colour, especially the reference to pink tinge versus light carnation colour. There is too little information on fruits/seeds to draw any conclusions.

The importance of scientific names, as with the curare example, is apparent in the examples of henbane in Gerard (Table 2.6). Yellow henbane is less clear from modern flora but it could be 'small tobacco' (*Nicotiana rusticana*).

Gerard (and others) had already noted that henbane of Peru was similar to native henbane. Indeed, the Latin name Hyoscyamus was being used for members of the *Nicotiana* genus long before being adopted by Linnaeus as a genus name for the similar black henbane. So a system of grouping or higher classification, linking plants with similar features, had begun, e.g. henbane was Gerard's genus-level description. He also noted that yellow henbane was called 'Dubius Hyoscyamus, or doubtfull Henbane, as a plant participating of Henbane and Tabaco'; therefore he identified it to have intermediate characteristics. Given what we know now about the evolutionary relationships between flowering plant species, was it appropriate to place these three species together?

Gerard was right – all three species of henbane are now placed in the family **Solanaceae**. This family, like the Apiaceae (which we met in Chapter 1), contains a range of useful and poisonous plants, e.g. potato (*Solanum tuberosum*), tomato (*Lycopersicon esculentum*), deadly nightshade (*Atropa belladonna*) and thorn-apple (*Datura stramonium*) (Figure 2.10). The Solanaceae family is characterised not only by a common set of morphological characteristics but also by biochemical characteristics relevant to their medicinal properties (discussed in Chapter 3). These biochemical characteristics are in turn determined by the genes of the plant. In fact, it is now routine for all plants and animals to be classified according to their DNA sequences, which has led to the development of molecular phylogenies showing the similarity or otherwise of different species and indicating common ancestry; in other words, as stated in Chapter 1, classification has an evolutionary basis.

You may have noted how Gerard's view of *Nicotiana tabacum* (henbane of Peru) as a medical wonder plant (Tables 2.3 and 2.6, e.g. Sacra herba) is somewhat different to its reputation today! The discussion of curare also cautions us against assuming that plants and their products are simply either toxic or beneficial. Many plants with toxic properties, such as *Strychnos* or *Taxus* species (Chapter 1), have often been found also to have a medical use. This raises major problems of health risk and ethical issues of use and prescription, which we explore in Chapter 4. The key to whether a plant is toxic or beneficial may lie in the dosage and method of application. Preparations of *Strychnos* taken orally help stop the muscular spasms in the digestive tract that cause diarrhoea. Injection of small amounts of products from certain *Strychnos* species and other plants (*Curarea*, see Chapters 3 and 5) cause relaxation of the muscles that is reversible. This was the basis of the use of these products in surgery (see Chapter 5). Injection of larger amounts of *Strychnos* (e.g. with a blowpipe arrow!) can cause death due to prolonged relaxation of the muscles that control

(a)

(b)

(c)

(d)

Figure 2.10 Examples of Solanaceae with medicinal or culinary value: (a) potato (*Solanum tuberosum*); (b) tomato (*Lycopersicon esculentum*); (c) deadly nightshade (*Atropa belladonna*); (d) thorn-apple (*Datura stramonium*).

breathing. Amerindians understood the principle of such dose-dependent effects for hundreds of years. They used *Strychnos* and similar plants as bush teas to help cure diarrhoea, and varied the composition and strength of the arrow poison to either kill an animal or temporarily relax it. Schomburgk recorded that the Maiongkong in northeast South America used a weak poison for shooting and stupefying toucans, which supplied the feathers used for their cloaks and other ornamental dress. After recovery, the birds could be used again to supply more feathers. (There is related material on dose-dependent responses in Topic 3, Section 2.1.) An interesting human parallel is provided by early accounts of the Spanish Conquistadors who invaded and conquered much of the New World in the early 16th century. Pedro Simon (1627) describing an attack on a 1548 Spanish expedition noted:

> They fought just with blowguns, into which they put tiny arrows dipped in a poison. These, even if they caused only a slight wound, deprived the victim of his senses for two or three hours, the time it took the Indians to flee, and afterwards he recovered without further hurt.
>
> (Pedro Simon, in Bisset, 1992)

Almost certainly this poison was a form of curare, with doses suitable for hunting small animals. Long before anaesthetists were manipulating the amounts of muscle relaxant and drug companies were altering the molecular structure of the active ingredients (Chapter 5), Amerindians were devising ways of using the same plant product for a variety of medicinal and hunting uses.

2.4 Whose intellectual property?

We have seen examples of how, in moving from oral to written (and ultimately electronic) communication, the shift of knowledge was from the individual and the local community to an international audience. This raises the ethical issues of **intellectual property rights (IPR)** and **patenting** of medicinal plants. Protection of intellectual property includes copyrighting of writing and music and trademarks. Within the domain of intellectual property are patents for inventions, which are defined as 'new and improved products and processes that are capable of industrial application'. The aims of IPR are generally laudable, as shown in the following quotation from a UK government-supported website:

C D

> Intellectual property, often known as IP, allows people to own their creativity and innovation in the same way that they can own physical property. The owner of IP can control and be rewarded for its use, and this encourages further innovation and creativity to the benefit of us all.

(intellectual-property.gov.uk)

However, there are clear difficulties in applying IPR, especially concerning medicinal plants. To what extent does intellectual property of medicinal plants rest with the individuals who first used them (such as the Macushi, although not necessarily used for their final purpose), the persons who first described the products or their use (such as the Schomburgk brothers or Waterton, without perhaps knowing the original source of that information, or the final use to which it might be put), the surgeons or medical staff who first trialled the products, or the laboratory scientists who first tested and developed the products as marketable drugs (perhaps unaware of the source of the original plant material)? Once in the public domain as either documentary information or pharmaceutical products, should plant products be legally controlled and demarcated as intellectual or other property, especially those that are derived from local indigenous knowledge?

Consider a parallel example. Do I (Michael Gillman) have the right to be named author of this Open University course text on medicinal plants? In writing this material, I am gathering information from a variety of sources. Some of those sources are based on opinions and information from other named and unnamed sources. My writing is read by other members of the S250 Course Team who give me comments. I consider those comments and I change the text. The text is edited by another person and finally printed. Should my name go on the book (do I own the intellectual property rights to that work?) or should it be the Course Team or should it be everyone who has made contributions to the generation of the content of the book? – a formidably long list. In one sense, it does not matter and, anyway, is unknowable. Intellectual activity is the product of an uncharted

E

series of conversations and debates (I learnt and paraphrased this from the quotation on the wall of a colleague's office) and I am simply the person who is producing a particular version of those conversations at a particular time. However, it would matter (to me!) if my income depended on it. If to earn my salary I have to show what I have produced, then I would want to have my name written on the material. Fortunately, this does not appear to be a requirement (yet!) at the OU. But it is the issue of money that drives so much of the contention over IPR and patenting. Patenting of medicinal plants or their products provides a legal base for the ownership of that plant or product and so ensures rights to income derived from that product, regardless of the inputs of others. When the income runs into millions of US dollars, the stakes for control are correspondingly high.

The issues of intellectual property rights reached new heights with the Trade Related Intellectual Property Rights (TRIPS) agreement of the World Trade Organisation, which came into being on 1 January 2005. Various commentators have noted the potential biases in TRIPS:

> It is an unbalanced treaty, based solely on enforcing patent rights worldwide as a mechanism to reward innovation […] It is hard to avoid the suspicion that the dogged advocacy of intellectual property law as the only way to stimulate innovation is more about maintaining world economic power than anything else.
>
> (Hubbard, 2004)

> The framework for the TRIPS patent system was conceived and shaped by the Intellectual Property Committee (IPC) of USA and industry associations of Japan and Europe.
>
> (Shiva, 2003)

Members of the IPC included several pharmaceutical companies: Bristol Myers, Johnson & Johnson, Merck and Pfizer. Shiva notes how this global agreement, which conflicts with some national agreements on patents (e.g. the 1970 Patent Act in India does not allow patents on medicines), can undermine health by inflating the costs of medicines. It also allows companies to control one of the final links in the long chain of development of medicines and thereby control the distribution and income from the final product. This is alleged to equate to 'biopiracy', effectively removing or negating the intellectual property rights of the originators of those products. Certainly, high financial stakes (recall the global estimate of billions of dollars in Extract 1.1) and political/corporate zeal help to generate monumental injustices. Two examples are selected below:

- The patenting of turmeric and rights to exploit it by a medical centre in Mississippi was revoked after appeals by the Indian Government that its properties were known to millions of Indians over many centuries.
- In 1866 the US Government asserted that, as a developing country, it had the right to the 'heritage of mankind' to assist its development. In 1999 the US Government threatened the South African Government over its copying of anti-AIDS drugs (although these were totally synthetic drugs rather than drugs based on natural products).

The concerns of developing countries were summarised in the following statement from the Indian Prime Minister, Indira Gandhi, at the WHO assembly in Geneva on 6 May 1981:

> Affluent societies are spending vast sums of money understandably on the search for new products and processes to alleviate suffering and to prolong life. In the process, drug manufacturers have become a powerful industry. My idea of a better-ordered world is one in which medical discoveries would be free of patents and there would be no profiteering from life or death.
>
> (Gandhi, cited in Shiva, 2003).

We will return to the issue of intellectual property rights and patenting of medicinal plants and their products in Chapter 5.

Summary of Chapter 2

The origins of medicinal plant knowledge are to be found amongst local indigenous peoples who over the last few thousand years have developed a detailed knowledge of their natural environment. Knowledge was (and in some cases still is) communicated orally.

Herbals from the Greeks onwards, including Dioscorides, helped to consolidate and disseminate medicinal plant knowledge. In Europe the Doctrine of Signatures guided medicinal plant knowledge, as in the case of St John's wort.

An example of indigenous plant knowledge is curare (or urari to the Macushi), the notorious arrow poison, a form of which later became used in surgery. Charles Waterton went in search of the Macushi curare in what is now southwest Guyana. Later, in the same region, the Schomburgk brothers described the key ingredient as being derived from the plant species *Strychnos toxifera*.

A second example of early medicinal plant knowledge was henbane, several forms of which were described in the 17th century in Gerard's herbal, with many medical applications. One of these plants was tobacco (like curare, also from South America), a member of the plant family Solanaceae which includes various species with medicinal properties.

The issues of intellectual property rights (IPR) and patenting were introduced in the context of the origins and dissemination of medicinal plant knowledge.

Question 2.1

Summarise (in about 200 words) the changes in communication of medicinal plant properties from oral traditions to the internet, focusing on the following aspects:

*   audience size
*   interactions between speaker or writer and audience
*   quality of information
*   frequency of updating.

Chapter 3   The medicinally active ingredients in plants

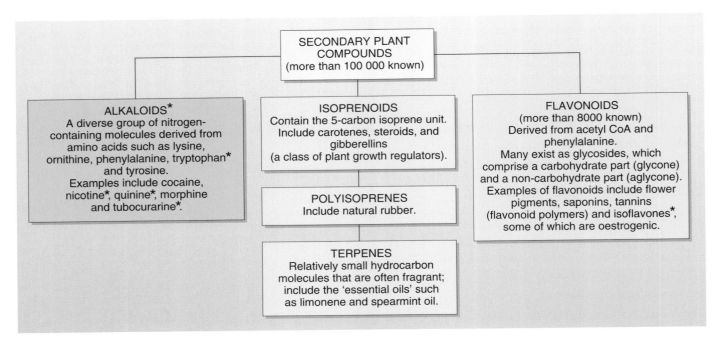

```
                        SECONDARY PLANT
                           COMPOUNDS
                    (more than 100 000 known)
```

ALKALOIDS*
A diverse group of nitrogen-containing molecules derived from amino acids such as lysine, ornithine, phenylalanine, tryptophan* and tyrosine.
Examples include cocaine, nicotine*, quinine*, morphine and tubocurarine*.

ISOPRENOIDS
Contain the 5-carbon isoprene unit. Include carotenes, steroids, and gibberellins (a class of plant growth regulators).

POLYISOPRENES
Include natural rubber.

TERPENES
Relatively small hydrocarbon molecules that are often fragrant; include the 'essential oils' such as limonene and spearmint oil.

FLAVONOIDS
(more than 8000 known)
Derived from acetyl CoA and phenylalanine.
Many exist as glycosides, which comprise a carbohydrate part (glycone) and a non-carbohydrate part (aglycone). Examples of flavonoids include flower pigments, saponins, tannins (flavonoid polymers) and isoflavones*, some of which are oestrogenic.

Figure 3.1   The main groups of secondary plant compounds. Names of compounds referred to in this and later chapters are identified with an asterisk. Secondary compounds may serve in plant defence or as attractants for pollinators or seed dispersers (pigments and fragrances). Figure A3.1 in the Appendix shows the structures of some of these compounds.

The medicinal activity of plant species may be traced to their biochemical composition, especially their **secondary compounds**, so called because they are outside plant primary metabolism which includes respiration and photosynthesis. There are various groups of secondary compounds (Figure 3.1) which can have many effects in the human and other animal bodies.

In the following section we will consider representatives of one of the main groups of secondary compounds, a diverse group of nitrogen-containing organic molecules called **alkaloids**. Alkaloids are found in many plant families and in other organisms, such as fungi and marine molluscs. The presence of alkaloids can be responsible for the bitter taste of medicinal plants.

3.1 The secondary compounds of curare plants and *Nicotiana*

The reason why plants such as *Strychnos toxifera* and *Nicotiana tabacum* have such extraordinary effects on the body is due to the presence of particular alkaloids in those plants. The detection and evaluation of secondary compounds is helped by comparative studies both within and between plant families. These studies have often been facilitated by independent indigenous knowledge. **Nicotine** (Figure 3.2) is an alkaloid found in the genus *Nicotiana* and also in some other members of the Solanaceae, such as **pituri** (*Duboisia hopwoodii*), and several other plant families. Pituri is found growing in arid parts of northern and western Australia and was used by Australian aborigines as a stimulant. Consumption of pituri is sufficient to achieve major alterations of consciousness.

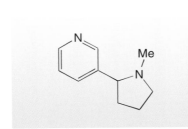

Figure 3.2 Structure of nicotine.

Plant leaves and stems were dried, powdered, mixed with alkali ash and rolled up into balls or sausage shapes and chewed. Pituri was used in a ritualistic context, especially by older men, with the knowledge passed down through generations in oral tradition. The older men had a monopoly on the knowledge and thereby controlled supply. The location of suitable *Duboisia hopwoodii* plants was a closely guarded secret, with information about drying techniques similarly guarded. Younger males attempted to obtain and process the plant, but failed due to lack of knowledge.

Unlike the distribution of nicotine in the Solanaceae, a fascinating feature of curare is that its active ingredients, also alkaloids, are now known to be derived from two unrelated woody vines in the genera *Curarea* and *Strychnos* in the families Menispermaceae and Loganiaceae respectively. Use of *Strychnos* as a source of curare seems to have been primarily by people northeast of the Rio Negro (Figure 3.3). In contrast, reports of curare derived from *Curarea* are from west and south of the Rio Negro. It was curare from this source that later became incorporated into the first muscle relaxant drugs (Chapter 5). Curare is therefore a tale of two vines and two sets of alkaloids, with similar effects but different evolutionary backgrounds. In fact, the situation for curare in Guyana may be a little more complicated. Chemical analysis of the Macushi curare brought back by Waterton also provided evidence that compounds derived from members of the Menispermaceae were similar to or the same as the *Curarea* alkaloid. This suggests that the Macushi either mixed curare made elsewhere with their curare or used locally collected Menispermaceae. Members of the Menispermaceae were used for medicinal purposes in Guyana in the mid-20th century, in a manner consistent with the mechanisms of curare action, e.g. for preventing diarrhoea.

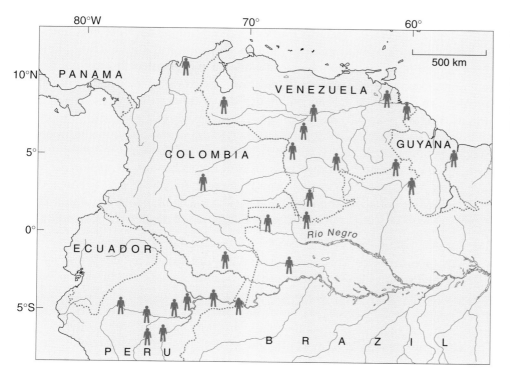

Figure 3.3 Distribution of tribes in South America known to have used curare in the 18th and 19th centuries. Most of the records from the northeast are of Loganiaceae-derived curare (although it was used elsewhere too).

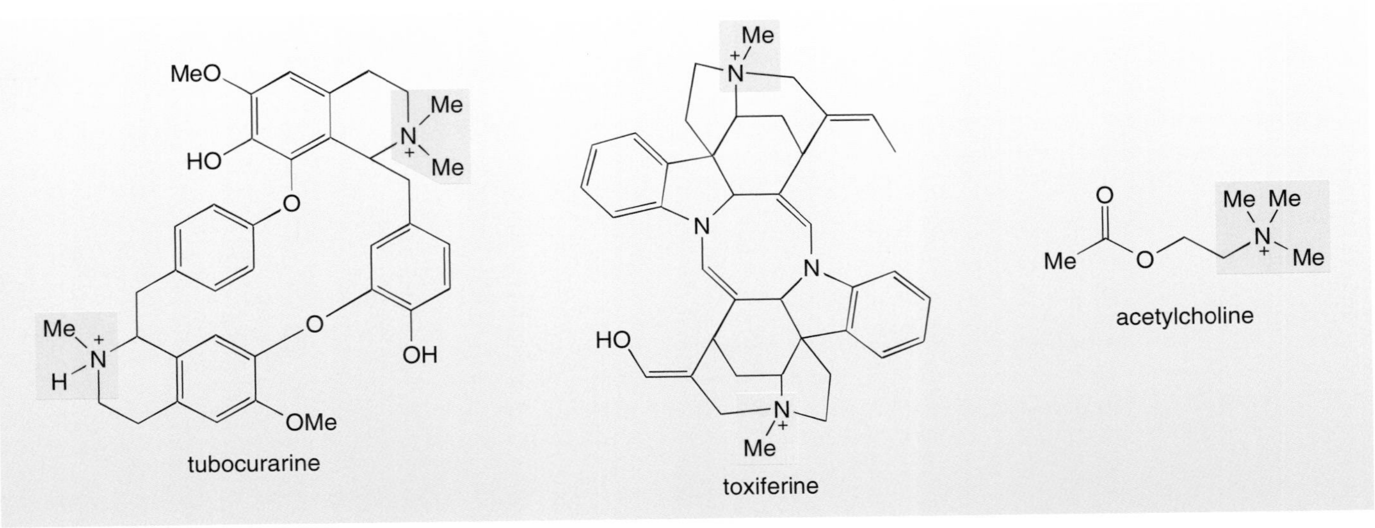

Figure 3.4   Structures of the alkaloids tubocurarine and toxiferine, and the neurotransmitter acetylcholine. The common structural features of tubocurarine and toxiferine that allow them to bind at the acetylcholine receptor are the positively charged nitrogen atoms linked to methyl groups (highlighted).

The active ingredient of curare derived from *Curarea* vines is the alkaloid **tubocurarine**, which was isolated by the chemist Harold King in 1935 from a dried plant specimen supplied by the British Museum. The active ingredients of curare from *Strychnos* vines include the alkaloid toxiferine. The chemical structures of these alkaloids are given in Figure 3.4.

The key to understanding the action of tubocurarine and toxiferine lies in parts of the molecules having structural similarity to **neurotransmitters**, which include **acetylcholine**, dopamine, noradrenalin and serotonin. In the case of those molecules resembling acetylcholine (i.e. acetylcholine analogues), the similarity centres on the positively charged nitrogen atom (Figure 3.4). Neurotransmitters are compounds that either pass across gaps (synapses) between nerve cells (neurons), or across synapses between a neuron and muscle, the neuromuscular junction. Consider acetylcholine, the neurotransmitter at the neuromuscular junction. Acetylcholine is contained in vesicles at the tips of neurons. When an impulse (action potential) reaches a nerve ending, the vesicles fuse with the neuron cell membrane and release their acetylcholine into the space between the neuron and the muscle cell (Figure 3.5). The neurotransmitter then binds to receptors on the muscle cell membrane, causing ion channels to open in the membrane of the target muscle cell, allowing calcium ions to flow in. This influx of calcium ions initiates a transient voltage change (action potential), along the length of the muscle cell, culminating in contraction of the muscle.

The curare alkaloids act by binding to the acetylcholine receptor molecules on the surface of muscle cells. This prevents acetylcholine from interacting with its receptor and so muscle contraction ceases. Note that although the tubocurarine binds to the acetylcholine receptors, it does not elicit a muscle contraction like acetylcholine. It is therefore known as an acetylcholine **antagonist**. Because acetylcholine receptors are found in many different groups of organisms (including insects, molluscs and vertebrates), the spectrum of species potentially affected by curare alkaloids is very broad. In humans, acetylcholine receptors

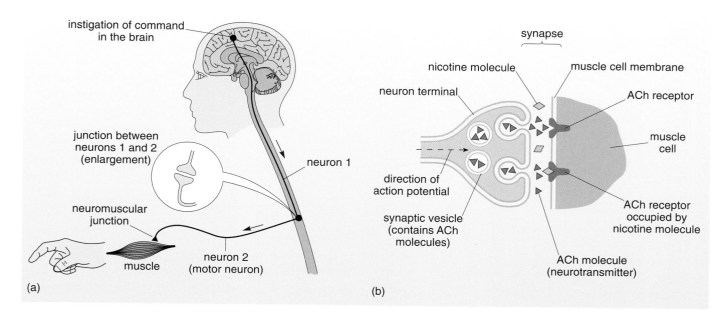

Figure 3.5   Acetylcholine and nicotine action at a neuromuscular junction. (a) Diagram showing the neural pathway from the brain to skeletal muscle (in this case a muscle controlling movement of a finger). (b) Schematic diagram of the neuromuscular junction, showing nicotine bound to an acetylcholine (ACh) receptor on the muscle cell membrane. Nicotine mimics the action of ACh (i.e. it is an ACh agonist), causing an action potential to be generated in the muscle cell membrane, resulting in contraction of the muscle.

are found in various parts of the motor nervous system (that part of the nervous system that conveys nerve impulses to muscles and glands).

Nicotine (Figure 3.2) has its effect at synapses where acetylcholine is the neurotransmitter (Figure 3.5). Like tubocurarine, it binds to acetylcholine receptors but it *stimulates* the postsynaptic cell, unlike tubocurarine which has an inhibitory effect. This stimulation in turn leads to increases in blood pressure and heart rate and the release of adrenalin. Therefore nicotine is an acetylcholine **agonist**. Indeed nicotine was used to discover some key features of the structure of the receptors in the target (postsynaptic) cell. Comparisons of the effects of nicotine with those of muscarine (see margin), which is derived from particular fungi, showed that there was one type of acetylcholine receptor in skeletal muscles and at neuron-to-neuron synapses (the nicotinic) and another in smooth muscle and cardiac muscle (the muscarinic). This reflects differences in the structure and function of the three types of muscle. Cardiac muscle is found in the heart and smooth muscle makes up the walls of structures such as blood vessels, bladder and uterus. Neither of these muscle types is under conscious control, in contrast to the skeletal muscles, attached to the skeleton.

Knowledge of the molecular structure of nicotine and muscarine helped elucidate the shape and structure of the receptor sites. This, in turn, helped in the development of drugs that selectively operated at these sites, as we will see in Chapter 5 with drugs developed from tubocurarine (a much more complex molecule than acetylcholine, Figure 3.4). The effects of plant compound (drug) action at receptors in the human body are discussed further in Chapter 4. The principle of alkaloids mimicking neurotransmitters is an important one in understanding the medicinal effects of plant secondary compounds (Table 3.1).

muscarine

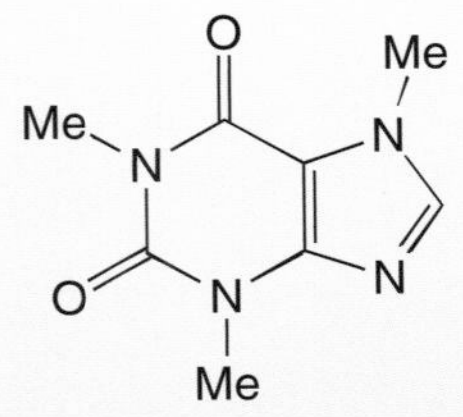

caffeine

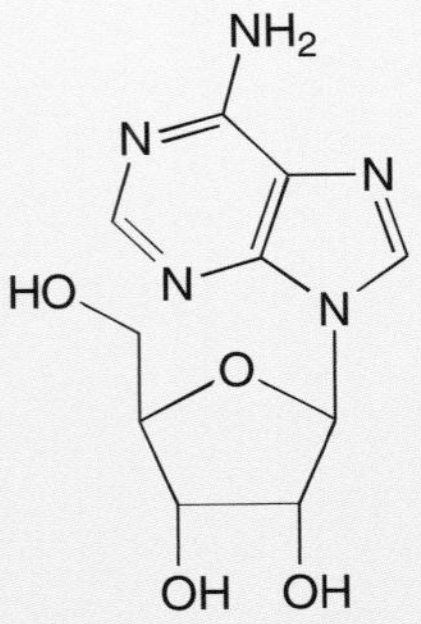

adenosine

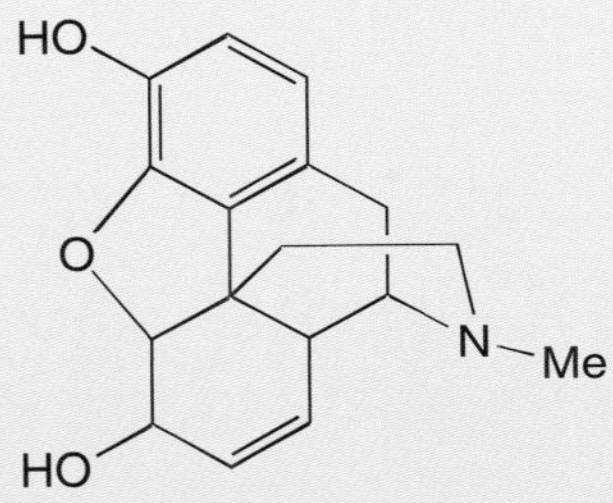

morphine

This includes hyoscyamine from the henbane (*Hyoscyamus niger*) discussed in Chapter 2, which mimics acetylcholine (Figure 3.6). Caffeine (see margin), another plant alkaloid, and the most widely used drug in the world, also works by blocking receptors in the central nervous system – in this case, the adenosine receptors. Adenosine (see margin) is a natural signalling molecule with a similar chemical structure to caffeine; it reduces the release of a wide range of neurotransmitters (including acetylcholine). Caffeine is an antagonist of adenosine, thereby increasing the release of these neurotransmitters and therefore acting as a stimulant. Another important group of alkaloids are those found in the poppy family (Papaveraceae, Table 3.1). These include some of the most powerful painkillers (e.g. morphine, see margin) and the most addictive substances, again including morphine and its derivative, heroin. The latter was originally formulated as a safe and non-addictive alternative to morphine and was especially valued as an addition to cough medicine. Its name, from the German *heroisch* ('heroic treatment') was registered as a trademark by the company Bayer in 1898, following its discovery in the UK in 1874.

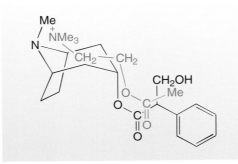

Figure 3.6   The structure of acetylcholine (red) superimposed on the hyoscyamine skeleton (black), showing how this alkaloid can mimic the natural neurotransmitter.

Interestingly, one of the antidotes to curare (and atropine) poisoning was another plant extract, **physostigmine** (Table 3.1 and Figure 3.7). In the 19th century, William Danielli observed the Efik people of West Africa using extracts of the Calabar bean (the fruit of *Physostigma venenosa)* in 'trials by ordeal'. During the 'trial', the suspect was given a poison to consume. Subsequent death signified guilt, whilst survival – usually because the suspect vomited the concoction up – signified innocence. Physostigmine works by inhibiting the enzyme acetylcholinesterase. If acetylcholine remains bound to its receptor at the neuromuscular junction, the muscle continues to be stimulated and contract. Acetylcholinesterase breaks down the acetylcholine, thereby freeing the receptor to bind more acetylcholine in response to another nerve impulse. Physostigmine functions as an antidote to curare poisoning because it allows any acetylcholine that is bound to the receptors to remain bound, thus blocking the binding of tubocurarine to those sites.

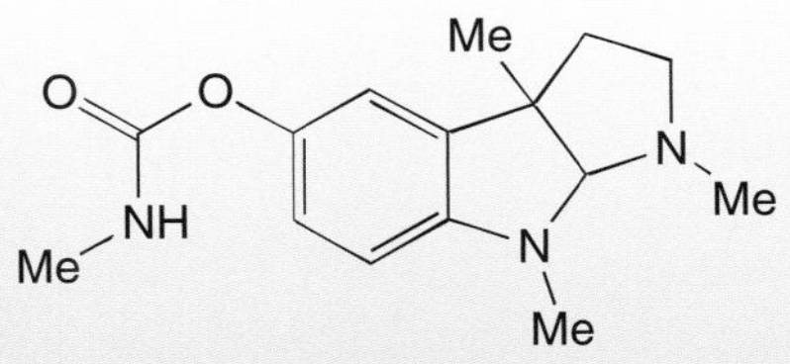

Figure 3.7   The structure of physostigmine, an inhibitor of acetylcholinesterase.

Table 3.1   Examples of plant alkaloids with effects on neurotransmission.

Alkaloid	Plant species	Plant family	Mode of action in human	Medical applications
atropine, hyoscyamine (these are the same compound)	*Atropa belladonna*, *Hyoscyamus niger**	Solanaceae	Block acetylcholine at muscarinic receptors (i.e. it is a muscarinic antagonist).	Counteract inhibitors of the enzyme that breaks down acetylcholine (acetylcholinesterase).
cocaine	*Erythroxylum coca*	Erythroxylaceae	Inhibits noradrenalin or dopamine uptake.	Used as a local anaesthetic.
ephedrine	*Ephedra vulgaris*	Gnetaceae	Causes release and mimics effect of noradrenalin.	Bronchodilator for asthma relief; nasal decongestant for hay fever.
morphine and other opium alkaloids, including codeine and heroin	*Papaver* (poppy) species	Papaveraceae	Block receptors in central nervous system (thereby blocking pain 'messages').	Analgesics (painkillers); dysentery treatment (ancient)
nicotine*	*Nicotiana** species, *Duboisia hopwoodii**	Solanaceae	Binds to acetylcholine receptors and acts as agonist (Figure 3.5).	
physostigmine*	*Physostigma venenosa*	Leguminosae	Inhibits the enzyme that breaks down acetylcholine (acetylcholinesterase).	Reverses effect of muscle relaxants; treatment for myasthenia gravis.
reserpine	*Rauwolfia* species.	Apocynaceae	Slows release of the neurotransmitter noradrenalin.	Antihypertensive, but has adverse effects so no longer used.
tubocurarine*	*Curarea** species	Menispermaceae	Blocks acetylcholine at nicotinic receptors (i.e. it is a nicotinic antagonist).	Muscle relaxant in surgery; antispasmodic; antidiarrhoeal.

* Compounds and species that are discussed in detail in the text.

Physostigmine derivatives are used to treat a rare but potentially fatal disease called myasthenia gravis (Table 3.1), an autoimmune disease in which the body produces antibodies to the acetylcholine receptors on the muscle cells. The receptors are thus destroyed by the immune system and although the body tries to compensate by synthesising new receptors, they cannot be produced in sufficient number. Inhibiting the action of acetylcholinesterase allows the acetylcholine more time to find a receptor to bind to and the length of time it remains bound is also increased.

Other plant-derived alkaloids may affect animals in different ways, interacting with key biochemical components such as nucleic acids and proteins, e.g. altering enzyme activity. These interactions may lend themselves to medical applications. For example, the protein **tubulin** has several functions in human cells (and in those of all other eukaryotes). One of these functions is in assisting cell division. Polymerised tubulin makes up the spindle structures that help align the chromosomes at the equator of the dividing cell and then separate them as the two new cells are formed. Disrupting the process of spindle formation is one way of stopping the growth of tumours. Several plant secondary compounds have been isolated that bind to tubulin and thereby prevent its polymerisation. These include taxol, which we met in Chapter 1, and the alkaloids **vinblastine** and **vincristine** (structures shown in Figure A5.7 in the Appendix), both of which were originally derived from the rosy periwinkle *Catharanthus roseus* (Table 2.1) in the family **Apocynaceae**, and subsequently developed and marketed as anti-cancer drugs (Chapter 5).

We now switch our attention to the value of secondary compounds to the plant.

3.2 Why do plants contain secondary compounds?

Why should plant compounds have evolved that act as neurotransmitters although plants do not have a nervous system? There are two types of scientific answer to this question. The first is that it simply reflects common metabolic pathways between plants and animals. Because plants and animals have the same (distant) common ancestors, they are expected to have some biochemical structures and processes in common. Of course, there are many major differences as well, but the commonality of structure and function may be sufficient that certain molecules that are active in a plant may also be active in an animal. This type of argument works well for fundamental metabolic processes, such as respiration, DNA replication and protein synthesis.

However, we have seen that the medicinal properties of plants are due to particular *secondary* compounds, i.e. those that are not part of the fundamental (primary) metabolism. Also, not all plant groups contain the same secondary compounds. Whilst some may have been lost during the course of evolution, it seems more likely that the compounds have evolved independently in different groups, such as the curare alkaloids in the Loganiaceae and Menispermaceae. There is also evidence that ecologically distinct groups of plants (e.g. long-lived versus short-lived) have different levels and types of secondary compounds.

So, the second answer is that there have been selection pressures for plants to evolve secondary compounds for defence purposes. This includes defence against herbivores and plant pathogens, e.g. certain fungi, bacteria or viruses (we will refer to herbivores and pathogens collectively as plant natural enemies). The natural selection argument is that plants with secondary compounds that have a defence function will survive better and leave more offspring (which themselves survive better and leave more offspring, i.e. have a higher biological fitness) than plants without those compounds. Thus a plant that contains a compound that interferes with the action of a neurotransmitter in an insect herbivore might cause that insect to stop or reduce feeding. This argument requires that there are sufficient numbers of plant natural enemies to warrant the metabolic cost of synthesising secondary compounds. There is no doubt that there is a huge abundance and diversity of plant natural enemies – the enormous richness of insect herbivores is an important example. These are in addition to the much more conspicuous vertebrate grazers and browsers. The interactions between plants and their natural enemies have also been played out over many tens of millions of years (and, more importantly for evolution, many millions of plant and natural enemy generations). These ideas are supported by direct fossil evidence. For example, rocks in the Dakota formations, laid down 97 million years ago during the Cretaceous period, contain the fossilised remains of more than 400 flowering plant species and the herbivores that fed on them. The fossilised records of insect damage such as leaf mining by moth larvae are so good that the plant-feeding insects can be identified to genus level and compared to species that are living today.

We are hypothesising that over tens of millions of years, many types of plant defence have evolved in response to feeding damage by herbivores such as insects. This has included chemical defences in the form of secondary compounds and physical defences such as spines. In turn, insects have evolved mechanisms of overcoming these defences, which have, in their turn, been counteracted by yet more effective plant defences, and so on.

The bright colours of the hawk-moth larva (caterpillar) in Figure 3.8 warns its natural enemies, e.g. birds, that it contain toxins, derived from the plant upon which it specialises (white frangipani, *Plumeria alba*). These toxins allow the larva to feed with impunity in the full glare of the tropical sun and onlooking potential predators. This phenomenon has been found in other species of moth and various other insect groups.

8 cm

Figure 3.8   A hawk-moth larva feeding on a leaf of white frangipani (*Plumeria alba*).

The fact that plant secondary compounds useful in medicine may also be plant defence compounds helps explain why they may also be toxic to humans. As we saw with the curare example, the reason that these potential poisons can be harnessed for medical use is because we can manipulate the dose and site of action of the natural plant product. Furthermore, drug development has led to alterations of the natural compounds such that the benefits can be retained without the harmful biochemical or physiological effects. Of course, drug development has its own costs. This is not merely in terms of labour and equipment but, as we hinted at the end of Chapter 2, also with regard to intellectual property rights, an issue that we will explore more thoroughly in Chapter 5.

Summary of Chapter 3

The medicinally active compounds in plants are identified as plant secondary compounds, e.g. alkaloids such as nicotine (found in members of the Solanaceae including pituri) and tubocurarine. Their effects are due to their similarity to naturally occurring signalling molecules in the bodies of animals, e.g. neurotransmitters such as acetylcholine, causing them to act as antagonists or agonists at neurotransmitter receptors.

Other effects of plant secondary compounds in animal bodies include interference with cell division by binding to tubulin from which the spindle fibres are formed. These compounds, such as taxol, vinblastine and vincristine have been developed as anti-cancer drugs.

Plant secondary compounds are thought to have evolved as defence agents against herbivores and plant pathogens, which explains why they may have harmful as well as beneficial effects in humans.

Question 3.1

Give two examples of potentially poisonous plant secondary compounds that have been used in medicine. Explain, from an evolutionary perspective, why such plant-derived compounds may benefit humans.

Risk and ethical issues of medicinal plant use

We have seen that plant-derived compounds may be beneficial or harmful, partly dependent on the method and dose of application. This raises serious issues for human health, especially when medicines are available without prescription. In this chapter, we explore the ethical issues and health risks associated with two groups of widely used plant products.

4.1 Wild yam

Although silphion has been lost, many plant species have been described from different cultures around the world that can be used as abortifacients or contraceptives. Whilst these uses have largely been replaced by clinical formulations or treatments, the use of plants that can affect the human reproductive system, especially that of females, is a substantial 21st century industry. These products can be bought via the internet and across the counter. Many of the plants used are those whose properties have been known for hundreds of years. Consider the example of **wild yam** (*Dioscorea villosa*, Figure 4.1). The genus *Dioscorea* is in the family Dioscoreaceae, named after Dioscorides. Wild yam products may contain a variety of additives (e.g. derivatives of liquorice, ginseng and soy – these species are discussed later) and are advertised as sources of progesterone. The wild yam products are stated to help with hormonal imbalances, reduce stress and mood swings and relieve

Figure 4.1 Drawings of *Dioscorea villosa* (wild yam) by Nicolaus Joseph Jacquin (1727–1817) reproduced from volume 3 in the series *Icones Plantarum Rariorum*. Jacquin was a botanist and chemist and a collector of ornamental plants in South America.

physical discomfort associated with either the menstrual cycle or the menopause. They also share features with other 'herbal' or 'natural' remedies in that they are advertised as 'organic', i.e. the contents are produced without the aid of inorganic fertilisers and synthetic pesticides. Extracts 4.1 and 4.2 below are from websites (listed in the References and further reading section) providing information about and/or selling wild yam products. We will examine the extracts, and the claims made about products, in Activity 4.1 which follows.

Activity 4.1

Allow 1 hour

Read Extracts 4.1 and 4.2 and then answer the questions (a) and (b) below. (Commentary text within the extracts is italicised.)

There are two aspects of Extracts 4.1 and 4.2 to unpick in this activity. First is the style in which they are written and second, whether there are any inconsistencies between the extracts. Both of these points are relevant to the course themes of communication and ethical issues.

(a) Briefly describe the styles in which the two extracts are written. You should note the use of personal views, statements of scientific evidence and any potentially conflicting commercial interests.

(b) Identify any inconsistencies in comments about progesterone and wild yam.

Extract 4.1 Advice on wild yam

The Aztecs and Mayans were the first to recognize healing properties in the root of the wild yam (*Dioscorea villosa*), a climbing vine. They used it to relieve pain. Years later, native Americans and early colonists made such a practice of treating joint pain and colic with this native North and Central American plant that it was, for a time, popularly referred to as 'colic root'.

Recently, wild yam has been promoted as an herbal alternative to hormone replacement therapy for menopausal symptoms. This claim is based on the inaccurate belief that the plant is a natural source of the female hormone progesterone. Although wild yam does contain diosgenin, a substance that can be converted into progesterone in a laboratory, it is not possible for the human body to make this chemical transformation.

There is no sound scientific evidence to indicate that rubbing wild yam cream into the belly, thighs, or any other soft areas will relieve symptoms of premenstrual syndrome (PMS) or menopause. In studies done so far, a dummy cream worked just as well. (If you want to try a natural progesterone cream that can be effective for menopausal symptoms, look for products that are certified to contain 400 mg of USP-grade natural progesterone per ounce.) Wild yam in other forms does appear to relax muscles and reduce inflammation, however. These properties, in part the result of substances it contains called alkaloids, explain why it seems to provide some relief from menstrual cramps, endometriosis, and digestive problems.

Although the wild yam plant produces large tubers that resemble potatoes, it bears no relation to sweet potatoes or true yams.

Extract 4.2   Hot flash – wild yam cream

by Beth Ellyn Rosenthal

Everything your doctor hasn't shared with you about the causes of PMS and menopausal discomfort [...] and the revolutionary natural solution.

Why women from 13 to 60 need the wild yam cream ... and some men too.

Ninety per cent of American women suffer from some type of menstrual problem. I suspect your PMS story can't be as bad as mine. But parts of our stories probably match. If you're like me, you've suffered from the day you had your first period: debilitating cramps; wild mood swings; super-sensitive breasts; pain that would make a line backer double over.

Fortunately, I've finally found relief. Now you can, too.

There follows a long testimonial about the physical and emotional difficulties of the author and the merits of wild yam cream, from which the following is a short extract.

Last year I got lucky. I learned about a natural form of progesterone made from a wild Mexican yam. This jar of peach-coloured cream looks, smells and feels like an expensive cosmetic. I rub one-quarter teaspoon of the sweet-smelling cream on different parts of my body twice a day during the second half of my menstrual cycle. (You'll read why the timing is so critical later.) My friend who turned me onto the cream promised this was the panacea I was looking for. I was willing to invest the meagre sum to find out.

I have to admit, at first I was sceptical. That a simple cream could take the pain away. Or exorcise my mood swings. Or cool the hot flashes. But this natural form of progesterone did all of that and more.

The personal experiences in the extract are supported by summaries of science taken from a book by Dr Betty Kamen, who is stated to have a PhD in nutrition. The extract later covers nutritional aspects, this time supported by the knowledge of the author:

Eating properly can go a long way in encouraging your ovaries and/or adrenal glands to produce more progesterone.

The author then states that:

Here I'm on firm ground

as the evidence is provided by the work of her company which

accurately measures your body's biochemistry. The test results are an Owner's Manual to your body that includes a road map that leads you back to health. The road map includes how to eat properly to fix the problems. I call it the grocery store solution, since you can find your 'cure' in the supermarket.

The testimonial concludes with the statement:

I swear by my wild yam cream. It has turned my life around – naturally.

The above text was accessed from a website supported by the Natural Health and Longevity Resource Center whose home page states:

Check back here often at the Natural Health and Longevity Resource Center for the latest in natural health, alternative medicine, holistic medicine, alternative therapies, herbal medicine, natural healing, herbs, fitness, medicinal herbs, nutritional therapies, complementary therapies, longevity research, physical health, mental health, and spiritual health. Many health experts agree that once the body is cleansed, nourished, and balanced, it has the ability to heal and recover from disease, as well as maintain health and long life. Now you can keep informed on some of the latest discoveries and healing methods from all over the world. Add this site to your bookmarks and check here weekly for news and updates!

The website cited includes the following advice on wild yam (amongst other herbal products in a 'Guide to Herbal Remedies'):

Wild yam has many effective uses. It is known to relax the muscles and promote glandular balance in women. Wild yam contains natural plant components known as phytochemicals which help the body balance hormone levels. Wild yam nourishes the digestive system and the nerves.

The following disclaimer is at the end of the list:

Nothing stated here should be considered as medical advice for dealing with a given problem. You should consult your health care professional for individual guidance for specific health problems. This page is for informational and educational purposes only, and is simply a collection of information in the public domain. Information conveyed herein is based on pharmacological and other records – both ancient and modern. No claims whatsoever can be made as to the specific benefits accruing from the use of any herb or nutrients.

C E

Extracts 4.1 and 4.2 comprise just a tiny fraction of the material available on the internet concerning wild yam and other herbal products. The websites quoted here represent part of the spectrum of views about herbal healthcare, which reflect many of the perceived polarities in conventional and alternative medicine. You may have a view on this, possibly representing your personal experience or that of friends or relatives. This debate is a complex one, reflecting a range of lifestyle choices. We will return to that debate later. In the comments on the activities, we have been careful not to say whether the material in the extracts is true or false. Even where statements are inconsistent, it may be that the product can work for one person but not for others or that the effects attributed to wild yam are produced by other ingredients in the cream. Similarly, a lack of scientific evidence does not mean that a statement is false (indeed, to falsify a statement we would need scientific evidence). More importantly, judgements about truth may be affected by perceptions of the presentation and source of the website. Part of our (sometimes implicit) evaluation of the information presented in such accounts is whether the source is a company marketing a product, a personal account of one person who has benefited (or not) from a product, a non-Governmental watchdog organisation reporting its views on a product, or a Government site offering advice. For some people, a Government website will be an attempt to control the masses, for others it will be a beacon of light amongst the uncensored websites. A second important influence on our perception of truth is the 'scientific' nature of the statements. The words 'scientific' or 'science' are frequently used to establish the veracity of information. This is because science is seen as indicating an objective pursuit. The inclusion or mere mention of scientific data, and especially the inclusion of primary sources from scientific journals, helps to make us feel that the statements are objective. Whilst scientific methodology is theoretically objective, science is undertaken by fallible and subjective individuals and the gathering and publishing of scientific data is a selective process. We will return to discussions of scientific method and objectivity at the end of this chapter.

To evaluate the information in these websites further, we need to consider the biochemical and physiological mechanisms underlying the effects of wild yam in the body. In so doing, you might consider whether there are any differences in the way that the science is sourced and presented here in this text in contrast to that available on websites.

4.2 Plant compounds that can affect the human reproductive system

Wild yam and its products are one of many groups of plant-derived substances aimed at women for controlling physical and emotional discomfort associated with the menstrual cycle and the menopause. The silphion phenomenon of miracle cure-all (Chapter 1) is echoed in much wild yam advertising (e.g. Extract 4.2). Although silphion may have been lost, we know that several species of Apiaceae have been used in birth control, regulation of the menstrual cycle and easing of childbirth.

■ How does this information help in understanding the possible mechanism of action of silphion?

▨ Because, as with the Solanaceae (see Chapter 3), we expect related plants to have similar secondary compounds. This means that study of existing members of the Apiaceae may shed light on lost members of that family.

A well-known example of an Apiaceae species used as an abortifacient or contraceptive is wild carrot or Queen Anne's lace, *Daucas carota*. (Queen Anne's lace is also used as a common name for other Apiaceae.) Extracts of other species in the Apiaceae have been found to inhibit the implantation of early embryos in rats. Later in this chapter, we will discuss the value or otherwise of using animal models such as rats for testing the effects of plant products on humans. Other members of the Apiaceae that are popular in commercial formulations include *Angelica* species, celery and the closely related ginseng (*Panax* species in the family Araliaceae, in the same order as the Apiaceae).

The reason why certain plant species have effects on the female reproductive system is that they contain molecules that mimic the activity of the **steroid hormones** that regulate the female reproductive system, most importantly **oestrogens** (e.g. oestradiol) and **progesterone**. As stated in Extract 4.1, wild yam is an important source of **diosgenin**, a secondary compound named after the scientific name of the plant (*Dioscorea*). Diosgenin, which is very similar in structure to progesterone, was used as a starting point for the synthesis of analogues of human steroid hormones (Figure 4.2). The term **phytoestrogen** is used collectively for plant compounds that mimic steroid hormone activity, i.e. not as the name implies, just those with oestrogen activity, but also progesterone mimics.

In Chapter 3 we discussed secondary plant compounds that can act as neurotransmitters. Although neurotransmitters and hormones are both chemical messengers, they differ in terms of the route and distance travelled through the body. Neurotransmitters cross the very narrow gaps (i.e. synapses) between nerve cells or between nerve and muscle cells, whereas hormones may travel long distances through the blood circulatory system.

Steroids, which include the steroid hormones, are a group of naturally occurring compounds in the plant, fungal and animal kingdoms. Steroids are often in the form of steroid alcohols, indicated by the name sterols; therefore those derived from plants are called **phytosterols**.

■   What does the occurrence of steroids amongst flowering plants, fungi and animals tell us about the evolution of this class of compounds?

▨   They are likely to have appeared early in evolutionary history (see discussion in Chapter 3 about ancestral origins of characteristics).

Steroid compounds have a common chemical structure but with a wide set of variations on this theme, some examples of which are given in Figure 4.2. In animals, the familiar compound **cholesterol** is an important intermediate in the formation of steroid hormones and serves other important functions too; in particular, it is a key component of cell membranes. All of the main steroid hormones (e.g. the oestrogens, progesterone and testosterone) are synthesised from cholesterol via the intermediate pregnenolone (Figure 4.3). Cholesterol is generally not found in plants. Instead, plants contain cycloartenol which is a precursor of other phytosterols, including stigmasterol and camposterol, via the intermediate β-sitosterol. These phytosterols have an important role in the structure of plant membranes (as cholesterol does in animals). The phytosterols, like their animal counterparts, serve as precursors to a set of regulatory molecules in plants which can affect gene expression, cell division and cell elongation. There is evidence for a crossover in function between plant and animal sterols. For example, β-sitosterol can be metabolized in the vertebrate body to pregnenolone and therefore perhaps to other hormones derived from pregnenolone. This illustrates one way in which phytosterols may affect levels of steroid hormones in the human body. Cycloartenol is also found in simple organisms such as yeasts.

Figure 4.2   Structures of some phytosterols (diosgenin, stigmasterol, cycloartenol and β-sitosterol), steroid hormones (oestrogens, progesterone, mifepristone or RU486), cholesterol (the steroid hormone precursor) and insect moulting hormone (ecdysone). (The characteristic steroid four-ring system is identified by shading.)

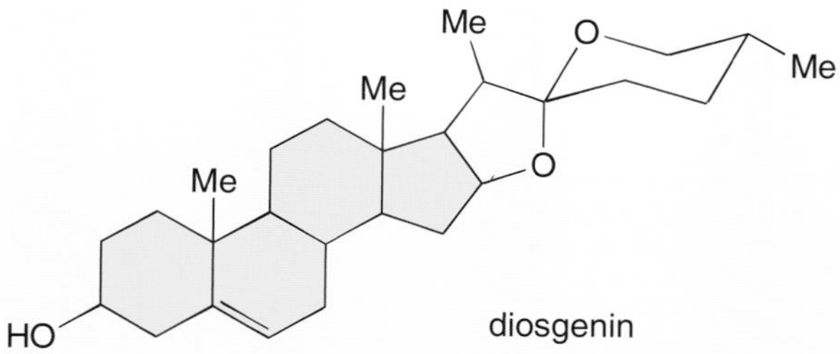

diosgenin

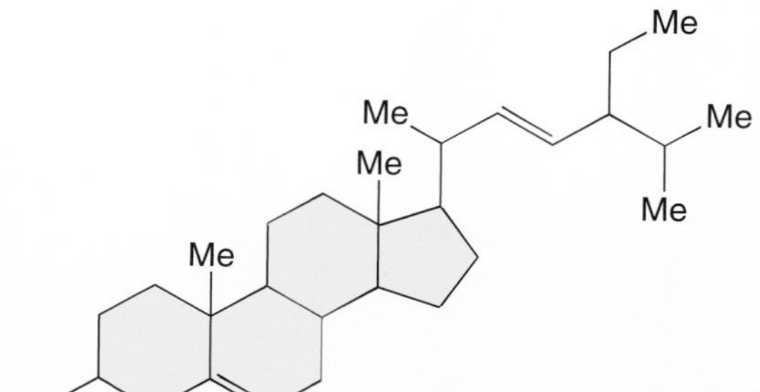

stigmasterol

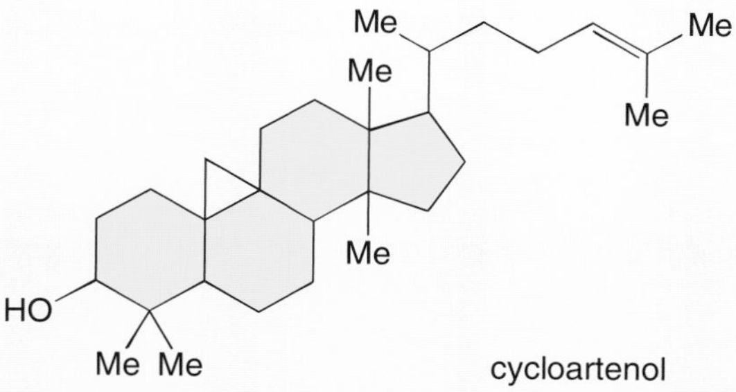

cycloartenol

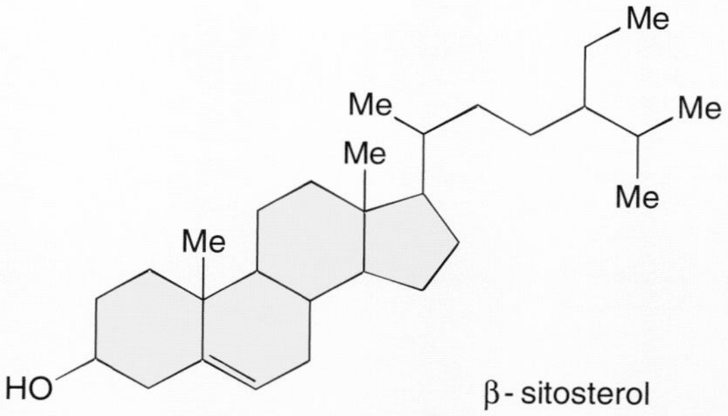

β-sitosterol

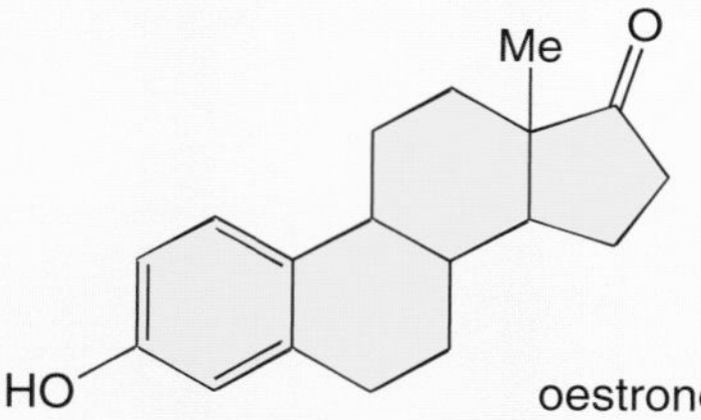

oestrone

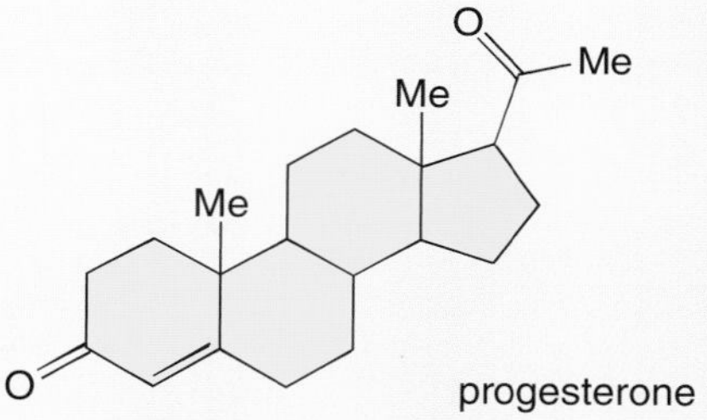

progesterone

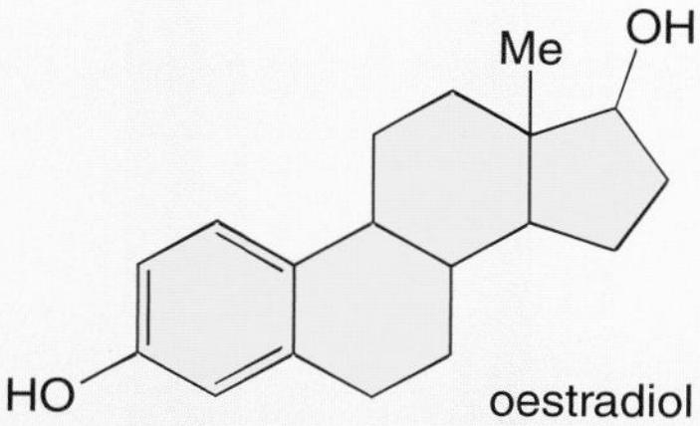

oestradiol

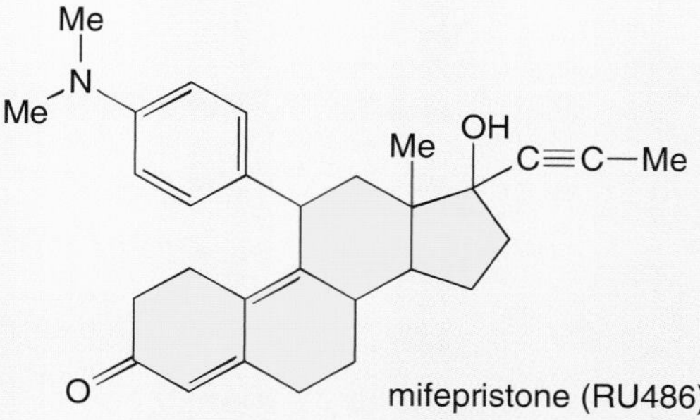

mifepristone (RU486)

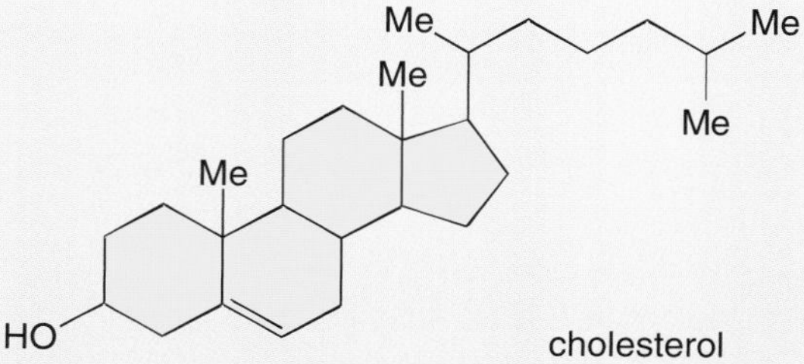

cholesterol

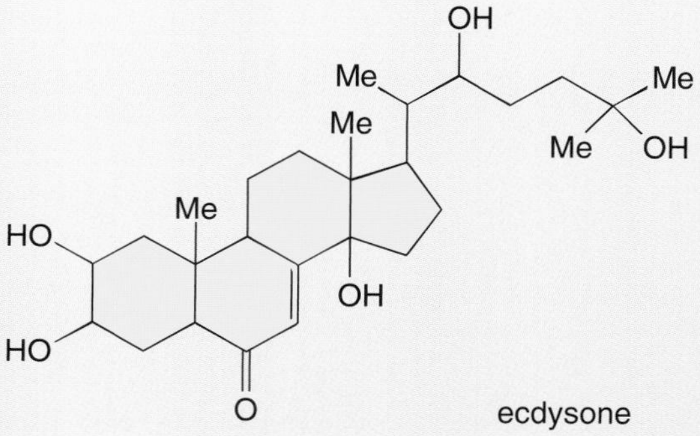

ecdysone

Figure 4.3 Summary diagram showing the main steps in the biosynthesis of steroid hormones from cholesterol.

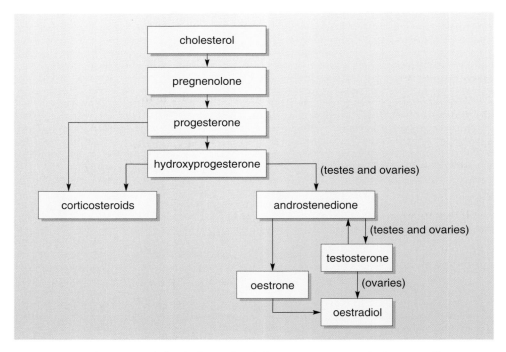

Progesterone has a special role in maintaining pregnancy and also contributes to regulation of the menstrual cycle. It is the principal hormone secreted by the large cells in the corpus luteum that differentiate from the granulosa cells in the ovarian (or Graafian) follicle following release of an ovum (egg cell). Progesterone is also found in the adrenal glands, testes and placenta and can act as an intermediate for the synthesis of other essential steroid hormones, such as the corticosteroids, which have a variety of effects in the body, e.g. anti-inflammatory and affecting water regulation. Oestrogens are formed in the ovary and, during pregnancy, in the placenta. They are also synthesised in the testes in males. (Note that testosterone is a precursor of oestrogens.) Oestrogens act on many tissues in the body and contribute to generally higher fat content of the female body and smoother skin. Oestrogen and progesterone regulate the menstrual cycle in the following way.

The menstrual cycle is taken to start with the onset of menstruation (Figure 4.4). This lasts for 3–6 days during which the superficial layer of the endometrium (lining tissue) of the uterus is shed. The cycle is divided into two phases (the follicular and the luteal). During the follicular phase, follicle-stimulating hormone (FSH) and luteinising hormone (LH), produced by the anterior pituitary gland (part of the pituitary gland, found in the middle of the base of the brain), act on the ovaries to promote the development of small groups of follicles, each of which contains an ovum. One of these ova develops faster than the others and forms the Graafian follicle, after which the others degenerate. Oestrogens are produced from within the Graafian follicle, stimulated by FSH. The oestrogens are responsible for the regeneration of the endometrium from day 5 or 6 to the mid-cycle. The oestrogens also have a negative feedback effect on the anterior pituitary, decreasing the release of FSH and LH. However, the increasing oestrogen levels then cause a sensitising of the LH-releasing cells of the pituitary, which results in a mid-cycle surge of LH. This in turn causes a rapid swelling and rupture of the Graafian follicle, resulting in ovulation. If fertilisation then occurs, the fertilised ovum starts dividing as it passes down one of the fallopian tubes to the uterus.

The increase in LH also causes the cells of the ruptured follicle to divide and develop into the corpus luteum (indicating the start of the luteal phase) which secretes progesterone. Progesterone is essential to the maintenance of pregnancy because it acts on the endometrium initiated by the action of oestrogen, making it suitable for implantation of a fertilised ovum. Progesterone has various other effects, including a negative feedback effect on the anterior pituitary, reducing release of LH. If a fertilised egg is not implanted, progesterone production stops and menstruation occurs. If implantation does occur, then the corpus luteum continues to produce progesterone, which prevents further ovulation by its effects on the hypothalamus and the anterior pituitary. The hypothalamus and pituitary gland have close structural and functional links. The hypothalamus secretes neurohormones which stimulate secretion of hormones from the anterior pituitary. The hypothalamus is also involved in control of (for example) body temperature and hunger. Understanding the hormonal basis of the menstrual cycle and pregnancy allows insights into how contraceptive and abortifacient compounds may act.

Oral contraceptives act by interfering with the relative levels of oestrogen and progesterone. The 'combined pill' gives a cocktail of oestrogen and a progesterone mimic (called progestogen) that alters the natural balance of these hormones such that the critical balance required for ovulation is never reached. The endometrium is also altered, making implantation less likely. In contrast, progestogen-only pills prevent ovulation by consistently increasing the level of progestogen, mimicking the pregnant state.

The action of abortifacients used in the early stages of pregnancy is illustrated by mifepristone (or RU486, Figure 4.2; RU refers to Roussel-Uclaf, the company that makes the drug and 486 is the shortened version of the original '38486' compound number first assigned to mifepristone in the Roussel-Uclaf laboratory). Mifepristone is used, with other medication, as an alternative to surgical termination of pregnancy. It does this by blocking the action of progesterone, binding more tightly to the progesterone receptor in the uterus than progesterone itself. However, it does not produce the biological effects of progesterone. Without these effects, the uterine lining breaks down and is shed, as in the menstrual cycle. Mifepristone also causes the cervix to open and leads to

Figure 4.4 (a) Relative levels of the steroid hormones oestrogen and progesterone during the menstrual cycle. M = menstruation. (b) The sequence of changes in the reproductive system during the cycle. (The dashed line in (a) shows what the progesterone level would be if fertilisation occurred.)

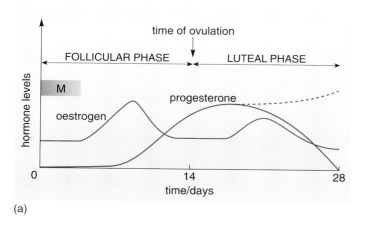

(a)

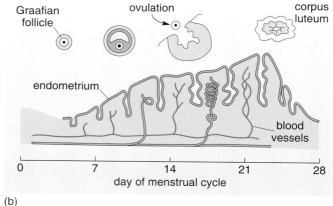

(b)

contractions which help expel the uterine contents. The pill can be used in the late follicular phase of the menstrual cycle (see Figure 4.4) as a post-coital contraceptive (the 'morning-after' pill).

■ In the example of the action of mifepristone, is it best described as an agonist or antagonist at progesterone receptors?

▨ It is a progesterone antagonist. Recall from Chapter 3 that agonists mimic the actions of neurotransmitters (or hormones in this case) and increase the levels of activity produced by those molecules. Antagonists reduce the activity, e.g. by blocking the receptor site but not activating it.

In fact, the action of mifepristone is intermediate between agonist and antagonist of progesterone, in that it has some properties of progesterone but also inhibits progesterone action. It is therefore known as a partial agonist.

Certain plant-derived compounds can act as contraceptives or abortifacients because they are structurally similar to oestrogen or progesterone (as is mifepristone, see Figure 4.2). Can they help in the relief of emotional and physical problems associated with the menopause or menstruation (as suggested in the wild yam articles)? This is plausible because the problems are associated with steroid hormone imbalance. For example, during the menopause, oestrogen levels fall due to decreased ovarian function. This has been addressed by **hormone replacement therapy (HRT)**, principally the use of oestrogens, but also with progestogens. Thus plant-derived compounds with oestrogenic or progestogen properties can *potentially* act in the same way as HRT. There is a large literature associated with potential costs and benefits (i.e. evaluation of the risks) of HRT. On the positive side, HRT can reduce menopausal symptoms (e.g. hot flushes and mood changes), reduce the risk of coronary heart disease and osteoporosis and may delay the onset of Alzheimer's disease. On the negative side, there may be increased risk of endometrial cancer (but the risk is reduced with progestogens), breast cancer, uterine bleeding and gastrointestinal symptoms (both due to progestogens) and increased risk of embolism (i.e. arterial blockage).

E

The difficulties of determining risk are well illustrated in this example of HRT. How can one balance reduced risk of heart disease with increased risk of breast cancer? Both of these risks can be quantified; for example, studies have suggested a 50% reduction in heart disease with HRT, yet a 20% increase in breast cancer up to the age of 60. But these are *average* effects over a large population. It is extremely difficult to say how one person will respond; indeed, it may be irresponsible to try to do so. However, at least such risks can be measured against known doses and treatment regimes. With plant remedies for menopause, such data are often not available and the molecules may be structurally and possibly functionally different. Therefore one is adding a whole set of new uncertainties to the uncertainties over HRT risk. We will revisit the risks of plant-derived therapeutic agents – and the ethical issues of advice surrounding them – in the remainder of this chapter.

The plethora of claims and counter-claims about the efficacy of herbal or natural remedies has lead to advisory and watchdog websites (see also the UK National

Health Service and MIND sites quoted in Section 4.3 and listed in References and further reading). These have been criticised as being part of the establishment but they generally offer a balanced view from a range of sources. An established and informative website from the USA is the aptly named Quackwatch site. Extract 4.3 from this site discusses wild yam cream and its role (and those of other natural products) with respect to HRT.

Extract 4.3 'Wild yam cream' threatens women's health

Timothy N. Gorski, MD

Many women are being encouraged to purchase and use 'wild yam cream' said to offer relief from premenstrual and menopausal symptoms. The preparation is made by a company called 'NATURAL efx' and is promoted with materials that include testimonials, the recommendation of a 'Dr Betty Kamen', and citations of medical literature purported to support the claims being made.

According to this promotional literature, 'hormonal imbalance' and 'oestrogen dominance' cause 'cramps, migraines, bloat, breast tenderness, hot flashes, can't lose weight, lack of energy, depression – mood swings, fibroid tumours, endometriosis – infertility, family history female-related cancer, foggy thinking, perimenopause, [and] losing height'. These conditions are said to be effectively treated by the application of the product twice daily. Also claimed is that the cream 'enhances libido, improves energy, stamina and endurance, stimulates the body's own production of oestrogen, progesterone, testosterone, [and] other hormones', and that 'women report [an] overall feeling of well being and euphoria'. It is also asserted that 'synthetic progestins [progestogens] have serious side-effects' whereas 'natural progesterone has none' and that the only reason the former is used is that it can be patented. Finally, even men are claimed to benefit from the product, which is said 'to help balance testosterone with no feminising effects'.

There is, of course, reason to suppose that hormones play a part in several of the conditions mentioned. For some of these conditions, though, this role remains uncertain or unlikely. It is certainly unwarranted to say that 'oestrogen dominance' is the cause of all the disorders mentioned and that a progesterone product can prevent, alleviate, or cure them. In the premenstrual syndrome, for example, double-blind controlled trials have demonstrated that progesterone supplementation is no better than a placebo. Also blatantly false is the claim that synthetic progestins are dangerous whereas natural progesterone is harmless. Progesterone in any form may cause side-effects. In addition, the major synthetic progestin now in use (medroxyprogesterone) has been off-patent for some time. It is generally preferred over progesterone – which is also produced synthetically – because it is much better absorbed when taken orally.

The more blatantly erroneous claim is that the Mexican yam, *Dioscorea villosa*, from which the cream is supposedly made, is a source of progesterone. It is not. In fact, the main hormonally active substances present in the plant are probably oestrogenic. Extracts of *D. villosa* do have significant amounts of the substance diosgenin. The plant is therefore very useful because in the lab – not in the human body – diosgenin can be used to synthesise steroid hormones including progesterone. Indeed, it was this discovery that led to the first commercially available oral contraceptives. The progesterone listed among the ingredients in wild yam cream may very well have been derived in this way via the test-tube from naturally occurring diosgenin. But that, of course, isn't mentioned in the product literature.

Also left unmentioned is the fact that, once introduced into the body by any effective means (including through the skin), the progesterone molecule can be metabolised to a wide variety of other compounds including oestrogens, androgens and even corticosteroids. Indeed, all of these vital hormones are the products of the continuous production of progesterone and its physiologic conversion in the ovaries, testes, and adrenal glands. Part of the usefulness of synthetic progestins, on the other hand, is that they are not subject to these biochemical pathways but can exert their desired effects until metabolised and excreted.

Thus, not only is there little reason to suppose that wild yam cream would be helpful for the medical conditions for which it is being promoted, but it doubtful that it ever could be as useful as synthetic progesterone.

The greatest danger posed by this product and its deceptive promotion is that it will lead many menopausal women to forego or even discontinue appropriate hormone replacement therapy (HRT). Although HRT is not for everyone (and few prescription medications are), hormone replacement has proven value in alleviating hot flushes, vaginal atrophy and other symptoms, as well as reducing bone loss and bone fractures. In fact, research suggests that the risks of combined HRT may attach more to the progestin component than to oestrogen. The fear and confusion created by promoters of wild yam creams and other unproven products are especially tragic since so many women already have trouble maintaining a consistent HRT regimen. The last thing American women need is another unproven 'natural alternative' promoted by a campaign of deceit at the expense of their life, health, and well-being.

Besides all these concerns, wild yam cream costs more. A month's supply costs about $27. A month's supply of the prescription drugs Premarin and Estrace costs $12 and $18 respectively.

Enforcement actions

The most outrageous promotion I have encountered is a 'Medical Recall Notice' mailing from 'Health Notification Service' of Henderson, Nevada. The official-looking contents purported to be a recall of all 'prescription oestrogens and progestins' because of 'severe and prolonged life-threatening side-effects'. According to this mailing, the 'indicated treatment' to be substituted was a 'natural progesterone cream' with 'no harmful side-effects', with the order form conveniently enclosed. FDA-approved progesterone medications, incidentally, do not make the false claim of 'no side-effects'.

In September 2000, the FDA warned the company owners (Roger J. and Debra L. Peeples) that it was illegal to suggest that their 'miracle wild yam cream' was useful in treating or preventing osteoporosis, symptoms of menopause, depression, premenstrual syndrome, breast cancer, postpartum depression, ovarian cysts, fibrocystic mastitis, infertility, or other diseases and conditions. In February 2002, the Illinois Attorney General charged the company and owners with violating the Consumer Fraud and Deceptive Business Practices Act and the Illinois Food, Drug and Cosmetic Act.

[Dr Gorski practices obstetrics and gynaecology in Arlington, Texas, and is president of the Greater Dallas-Fort Worth Council Against Health Fraud.]

You will see that there is an interesting similarity in the statement concerning wild yam promotion in the first two paragraphs of Extract 4.3 to the wild yam eulogy in Extract 4.2 (Extract 4.2 was found independently of Extract 4.3). The same expert and the same method of support (testimonial) are cited for a wild yam product. The Quackwatch extract also states that wild yam is not a source of progesterone (as did Extract 4.1). Indeed it may have oestrogen-like properties. Perhaps the most important risk and ethical issue identified in the article is that women may fail to take medical advice and withdraw from established medication programmes (e.g. hormone replacement therapies). This is not to say that conventional programmes, which perhaps include prescription of synthetic drugs, are perfect or have all the answers for all individuals. However, there is a risk to health if people are being encouraged to self-diagnose and self-prescribe. Being well informed is important, but we cannot all be experts in all things medical. Furthermore, self-prescription is being done with products that contain a vast array of different ingredients in unknown amounts. Many of the plant products contain phytoestrogens sourced from members of the Apiaceae and Leguminosae, including soy (*Glycine max*), black cohosh (*Cimicifuga racemosa*), clover (*Trifolium* species), *Panax ginseng*, dong quai (*Angelica sinensis*) and liquorice root (*Astragalus* species). Several of these species in the family Leguminosae (soy, clover, liquorice) are good sources of **isoflavones** which mimic the steroidal structure of oestrogens in female vertebrates (Figure 4.5)

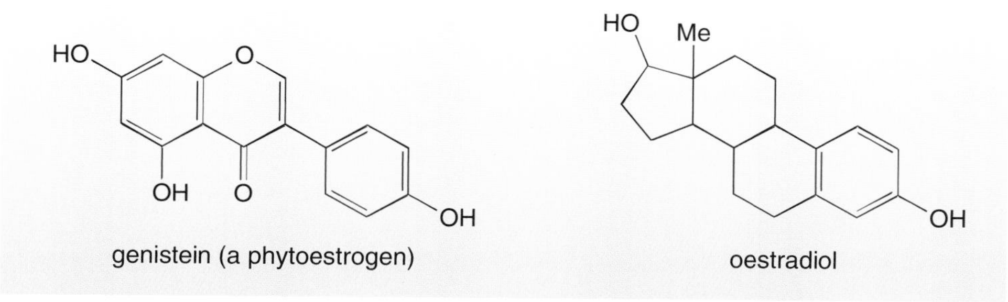

E

genistein (a phytoestrogen)   oestradiol

Figure 4.5   Structure of the soy isoflavone, genistein and the oestrogen, oestradiol. *Note*: The oestradiol structure shown in Figure 4.2 has been turned through 180 degrees to show the structural correspondence.

E   Another important ethical issue is that people are being encouraged to think that because the sources are natural there is less risk to health.

- ■   What lesson from Chapter 3 about the reasons why plants have secondary compounds might suggest caution in the use of 'natural' remedies?
- ▣   That many secondary compounds have evolved as agents of defence against herbivores (which include humans!).

So have phytoestrogens evolved due to selection pressures from herbivores and plant pathogens?

- ■   What effect might a phytoestrogen have on a herbivore?
- ▣   The herbivore's hormonal regulation might be affected.

In fact, it seems that phytoestrogens can act as defence compounds by altering the development of herbivores. The insect hormone ecdysone, which controls insect moulting, has a very similar structure to cholesterol (see Figure 4.2). Structural analogues/mimics of ecdysone are found in yew (*Taxus baccata*) and many other plants, especially gymnosperms and ferns. Consumption of sufficient quantities of plant-derived ecdysone mimic by insect larvae leads to alterations in their development, and ultimately death.

Herbivorous vertebrates are also known to be affected by phytoestrogens. In Australia, the presence of isoflavones in clover (*Trifolium* species) has caused sheep to fail to give birth. In the 1970s it was estimated that one million sheep per year failed to produce lambs in Australia due to 'clover disease'. Thus, plants are able to regulate the numbers of their natural enemies through possession of phytoestrogens. Indeed, it appears that this defence strategy has evolved to such an extent that some species contain exact copies of human sex hormones (e.g. testosterone in Scots pine, *Pinus sylvestris*; oestradiol in French beans, *Phaseolus vulgaris*).

In conclusion, by self-prescribing natural phytoestrogen compounds we are experimenting with compounds that have evolved to harm the development and hormonal regulation of herbivores. This is no different in principle from experimenting with other secondary defence compounds such as nicotine, heroin, cocaine and caffeine.

The risks of phytoestrogens for women are not only from approved (or otherwise) medicinal sources but also because of the widespread occurrence of phytoestrogens in foodstuffs and as contaminants of water bodies. For example, it has been shown that β-sitosterol (Figure 4.2), present in high concentration in wood pulp effluent, may function as a steroid hormone mimic and affect endocrine function (i.e. hormone production) in wildlife. Another study with rats suggested that the same compound may compete with cholesterol and thus interfere with the synthesis of steroid hormones, creating a prenatal environment with low levels of oestrogens. The authors also suggest that the hormonal environment during pregnancy may affect the behaviour in adult animals.

4.3 St John's wort

In Chapter 2 we discussed the origins of the use of St John's wort and mentioned a modern application for the treatment of depression. Here we will discuss evaluation of the costs and benefits associated with use of St John's wort today, developing the ideas beyond the wild yam example by considering the role of clinical trials and scientific method. St John's wort and its products are widely available for purchase without prescription in the UK (e.g. Figure 4.6) and elsewhere.

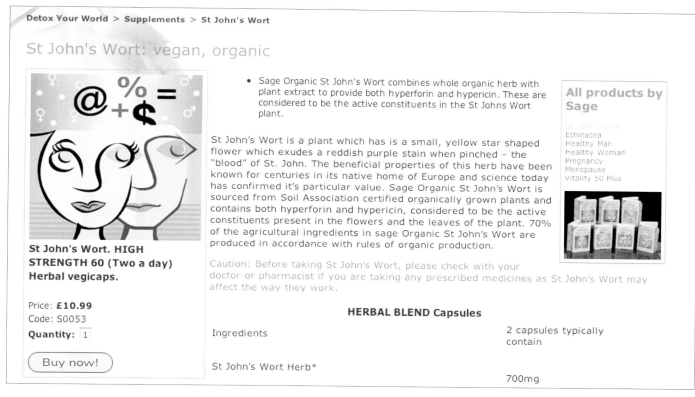

Figure 4.6   Publicity and background information relating to a St John's wort product.

■   What similarities do you notice between the advertising in Figure 4.6 and discussion of wild yam products in Section 4.1?

□   The support of 'science' for its (medicinal) value and its 'organic' source.

But does science really endorse the product in this manner? The following extract from the website maintained by the UK charity MIND considers the value of St John's wort, especially in the treatment of depression, and outlines some of the scientific evidence.

Extract 4.4 St John's wort – *Hypericum perforatum*

Written and updated by Katherine Darton

What is St John's wort?

St John's wort is a herbal remedy that has been known for thousands of years, but has recently been produced in tablet form and extensively marketed as a treatment for depression. Many people are under the impression that as herbal remedies are 'natural', this means that they are completely safe and free of side-effects. This is not the case: many herbs are very poisonous (hemlock is an obvious example), while other plants are poisonous in some parts and safe in others (e.g. the potato). Extracts from poisonous plants may make very useful medicines when used in the right way (e.g. digitalis, a heart drug that comes from foxglove). And of course there are some herbs that are both harmless and useful as medicines.

St John's wort is a plant named after St John the Baptist, whose feast day, June 24th, occurs when daylight in Europe is longest and the plant is in full bloom. Its five yellow petals resemble a halo, and its red sap symbolises the blood of the martyred saint.

St John's wort has been used as a folk medicine for many hundreds of years, particularly for healing wounds. Its antibacterial properties were reported scientifically in 1959 and 1971, when the active antibacterial substance, called hyperforin, was extracted and analysed. In medieval times St John's wort was used for 'driving out the inner devil'. Paracelsus (c. 1525) recommended it for hallucinations and 'dragons', as well as for healing wounds.

Tablets made from a standardised extract of St John's wort have been extensively researched in Germany since the early 1980s, and in recent years it has come on to the market as a herbal remedy, available from health food shops, to be used for mild to moderate depression. It was not found helpful for severe depression, and this was confirmed in more recent reports in America.

Scientific studies of the herb suggest that it acts to increase the activity and prolong the action of the neurotransmitters serotonin and noradrenalin, in a similar manner to standard antidepressants, but with many fewer reported side-effects.

The German trials appear to have used a daily dose of total extract, ranging from 0.4 mg (400 µg) up to 1000 mg (1 g). Currently the recommended daily dose is about 900 mg of total extract.

As with other antidepressants, St John's wort may take two to four weeks to begin to take effect.

There is also a product available combining St John's wort with other herbs as Hypericum Complex. This contains lemon balm (*Melissa officianalis*) and hops (*Humulus lupulus*), which are both sleep-inducing herbs. The complex is therefore suggested for people with depression who have difficulty sleeping.

Is it always safe to take St John's wort?

There are no listed contraindications for St John's wort (situations when it should not be used). It should be used with caution during pregnancy and while breast-feeding because there is no information on its safety in these conditions. Patients with a diagnosis of manic depression should use it with caution, since, as with all antidepressants, its use is associated with 'switching', or moving rapidly from a low to a high mood.

Is it safe to take St John's wort with other drugs?

People who are taking any other medicine should always seek professional advice before combining it with St John's wort.

You should not take St John's wort at the same time as SSRI* or MAOI* antidepressants. (It has been made a prescription-only drug in the Irish Republic because of anxieties about its possible similarity to MAOI antidepressants.)

St John's wort may prolong the effects of some sleeping pills and anaesthetics. If you are to receive an anaesthetic, you should tell the anaesthetist if you are taking St John's wort.

It also reduces blood levels of oral contraceptives, increasing the risk of pregnancy and breakthrough bleeding.

The British National Formulary 40th edition (September 2000) listed for the first time significant interactions between St John's wort and several other types of medicines.

Are there any side-effects?

The most commonly reported side-effects include gastrointestinal symptoms (such as nausea, vomiting, diarrhoea), allergic reactions, fatigue, dizziness, confusion, and dry mouth in a small percentage of patients. Another rare side-effect is photo-sensitisation – increased sensitivity to sunlight. This is associated with high doses, but people taking it should increase their sun protection and avoid strong sunlight.

The website concludes with details of helpful organisations and sources, which are not included here.

[Mind Information Unit, updated September 2002.]

■ What does the scientific evidence cited in Extract 4.4 suggest about St John's wort as medicine for treating depression?

  It seems to increase the activity and prolong the action of two neurotransmitters (serotonin and noradrenalin), which may help with less severe depression.

* SSRI = selective serotonin reuptake inhibitor; MAOI = monoamine oxidase inhibitor.

The two examples quoted below give an idea of the type of studies undertaken to assess the effects of St John's wort:

> An overview of 23 clinical studies in Europe found that extracts of the plant might be useful in cases of mild to moderate depression. The studies, which included 1,757 outpatients, reported that St John's wort was more effective than a placebo (a 'dummy' pill designed to have no effect) and appeared to be as effective as standard antidepressants.
>
> (Linde *et al.*, 1996)

> The results of a study in 11 academic medical centres in the United States with 200 adult outpatients with major depression, found that St John's wort, when compared with placebo, was not effective for treating major depression.
>
> (Shelton *et al.*, 2001)

Superficially these two studies, published in top medical journals in the UK and USA respectively, appear to give different results. However, the first is a study of studies (termed a meta-analysis) concentrating on mild to moderate depression whilst the second focused on major depression. These trials are characterised by large sample sizes, using human subjects and placebos. These are all parts of a wider **scientific method** that allows objective tests of particular hypotheses or questions. In this case, our hypothesis might be that St John's wort is an effective treatment for depression. Often the best starting point is a null hypothesis of no difference or no effect. In other words, we would hypothesise that St John's wort has no effect on depression. We can then undertake a study to test our null hypothesis, gathering various data and doing statistical tests that allow us to either accept or reject the hypothesis at a certain level of probability. (Box 1.7 in Topic 1 introduced the ideas of statistical probability.) If the original null hypothesis is rejected – in other words, St John's wort *does* have an effect on depression – then we would move on to another null hypothesis, e.g. that St John's wort has no effect on severe depression. (In reality we might consider several null hypotheses together in one study.)

So how would we go about designing a **clinical trial** (i.e. a scientific experiment using humans) to test the effect of St John's wort on depression? Note that these ideas apply to a whole range of scientific experiments. First we need a large number of humans with reported symptoms of depression.

■ Why do we need a large number of individuals?

▦ Because there will be variation between individuals which, with small numbers, may obscure any effects of St John's wort, and because we need some individuals to take St John's wort and some not to take it, i.e. to act as a control group.

■ How could you remove some of the variation between individuals?

▦ By selecting individuals that are the same age, sex, weight, occupation, etc. Alternatively, you may choose to include this variation in your study. (You can do this either by measuring age, weight, etc. and including the measurements in your statistical analysis, or by making sure there are similar numbers of individuals in these different categories and including the categories in the statistical analysis.)

Even if you have allowed for the observed variation, you still may need a large number of individuals in each group to allow for other environmental and genetic variation. (One reason why studies with identical (monozygous) twins are so popular is that they help to remove the genetic variation in a study.)

Now imagine that we split the individuals into two groups, one of which receives the St John's wort. It is important to select the individuals at random for each group to avoid any subjectivity in choice. We might choose to test all the individuals for symptoms of depression prior to administering St John's wort. This will also help to allow for individual variation, as we can test the changes in the same individuals before and after the experiment. Note that we will have to develop a standardised method of testing, which may include biochemical measurements and behavioural observations. The group not receiving St John's wort are given a placebo – a dummy pill. The real and dummy pills may be administered over a course of several days or weeks and testing undertaken during and after the course.

- Why is it important for the non-St John's wort group to take a dummy pill?

  Because we are dealing with depression, and may be especially interested in less severe forms of depression, it is possible that those who receive a pill will feel better because they know that they are receiving a pill. If they do not receive a pill, they will know they are not receiving any treatment! Placebo studies are standard in many types of clinical trial.

Furthermore, the administering of pills needs to be 'blind', i.e. the recipient must not know which type of pill they are receiving. Even better is a '**double blind**' study, when the people administering the pill – and, ideally, also those assessing the patients – do not know which type it is (and therefore could give no unintentional clues to the recipient).

At the end of the study, the data are gathered together and subjected to one or more statistical analyses. This will allow us to accept or reject the null hypothesis (of no difference) at a certain level of probability. Indeed, any scientific study or experiment that tests a hypothesis will ultimately produce a probability value associated with a statistical test. Thus a rigorous scientific study should never report that there is or there is not a particular effect, instead it should say that the probability that the observed data are consistent with the null hypothesis is P. (Note that the method makes the initial *assumption* that the null hypothesis is correct.) If P is small, typically less than 0.05, the data are not regarded as consistent with the null hypothesis and so it is rejected. It may be that P is close to 1 or to 0 but, especially with biological experiments, it will never be 1 or 0. If it is, then it is likely that the study was trivial. For example, the null hypothesis that humans do not have four eyes would be accepted with $P = 1$! So, in all these studies you should check the probability value. This is especially useful in assessments of risk. (Recall the discussions of probability and confidence levels in Topics 1 and 2.) A good way of remembering what the P value means is to think of it as a 'plausibility value' so that 'small plausibility means the data do not fit very well with the assumption that the null hypothesis is true' (Petrucelli *et al.*, 1999).

E

As you will appreciate, it is quite difficult to construct this type of clinical trial, especially when dealing with human emotional states. In discussing scientific methodology applied to humans, it is appropriate to consider the use of non-human animal studies. There is clearly a wide range of strongly held views on the subject of animal testing. (The use of animal 'models' in studying disease was discussed in Box 1.2, Topic 1.) Whilst it is true that much medical knowledge has come about due to studies on animals, it is also true that animals have been subjected to much unnecessary study. This is especially the case when testing for products that are peripheral to the needs of humans. In thinking about animal studies for addressing medical conditions, we must ask whether the biochemical, physiological or behavioural results are really transferable to humans; whether there exist any viable alternatives (such as tissue culture or computer models); and whether the seriousness of the human condition merits the use of animal testing. Inevitably there is subjectivity in answers to the last question, but at least the question should be asked.

So where does all this scientific evidence leave us in the assessment of risk (costs and benefits) of products such as St John's wort? Another website (that of the Norfolk and Waveney Mental Health Partnership), produced by medical practitioners, contains information on St John's wort and a comment on the risks. It states that 'the recommended dose for treating depression is 300 mg taken three times a day'.

It also states, in support of the above evidence, that:

> Research has so far found St John's wort to be useful in the treatment of mild to moderate depression. It has, however, not been found to be particularly helpful in severe depression.

The common side-effects of dizziness, stomach upset and confusion are noted, along with rarer side-effects of rashes or itches and photosensitivity. The site is especially cautious about the possible effects of St John's wort (and indeed any medicine) during pregnancy:

> It is important to consider that there will be a risk to you and your child from taking a medicine during pregnancy but also a possible risk from stopping the medicine, e.g. getting ill again. Unfortunately, no decision is risk-free. It will be for you to decide which is the least risk. All we can do here is to help you understand some of the issues, so you can make an informed decision.

Further details are given about the effects of medicine in pregnancy. The site continues:

> Very few medicines have been shown to be completely safe in pregnancy and so no manufacturer or advisor can ever say any medicine is safe. They will usually advise not to take a medicine during pregnancy, unless the benefit is much greater than the risk. In the UK, there is the NTIS (National Teratology Information Service) who offer individual risk assessments. However, their advice should always be

used to help you and your doctor decide what is the risk to you and your baby. There is a risk from taking the medicine and a risk should you stop a medicine, e.g. you might become ill again and need to go back on the medication again. The advice offered here is just that, i.e. advice, but may give you some idea about the possible risks and what (at the time of writing) is known through the medical press. It may be helpful to know that in the USA, the FDA (Federal Drug Administration) classifies medicines in pregnancy in five groups:

A = Studies show no risk, so harm to the unborn child appears only a remote possibility.

B = Animal and human studies indicate a lack of risk but are not fully conclusive.

C = Animal studies indicate a risk but there are no safety data in humans.

D = A definite risk exists but the benefit may outweigh the risk in some people.

X = The risk outweighs any possible benefit.

St John's wort is not classified. Little is known about it in pregnancy so until we know more, St John's wort is currently best avoided in pregnancy. You should still seek personal advice from your GP, who may then if necessary seek further specialist advice.

The striking point here is that, especially with sensitive personal issues such as pregnancy, the NHS will advise based on the **precautionary principle** (see the *Introduction to the course*). In other words, whatever the size of the risk (and particularly where it has not been assessed), the safest thing to do is not to take that risk. In this case, the responsibility for decision making is devolved to the individual.

D

Finally, why are we buying products whose treatment effects are dubious and that may have harmful side-effects? One view is that products such as St John's wort, in common with many non-prescription plant products, pander to the needs of a dependent society. Many of us overuse legal recreational drugs including alcohol, caffeine and nicotine. Many people in developed countries take too little exercise and have poor diets (many people in developing countries do not have the choice). Some of us are aware that this is bad for us so we move to natural healthcare products or supplements to compensate. This is not to decry the value of many medicinal plant products, but rather to observe that the impetus for use of non-prescription products is not one of medical necessity but lifestyle.

To close this chapter, another extract from an article on the Quackwatch website is included. It is an entertaining and informative read which touches on many of the issues in this chapter and covers wider scientific issues such as methodology.

Extract 4.5 Distinguishing science and pseudoscience

Rory Coker, PhD   Physics Department, University of Texas

The word 'pseudo' means *fake,* and the surest way to spot a fake is to know as much as possible about the real thing, in this case science itself. When we speak of knowing science we do not mean simply knowing scientific facts (e.g. the distance from earth to sun; the age of the earth; the distinction between mammal and reptile, etc.) We mean that one must clearly understand the nature of science itself – the criteria of valid evidence, the design of meaningful experiments, the weighing of possibilities, the testing of hypotheses, the establishment of useful theories, the many aspects of the methods of science which make it possible to draw accurate, reliable, meaningful conclusions about the phenomena of the physical universe.

However, the media provide a continuous bombardment of sheer nonsense, misinformation, fantasy and confusion – all proclaimed to be 'true facts'. Sifting sense from nonsense is an almost overwhelming job.

It is therefore useful to consider some of the *earmarks* of pseudoscience. The substitution of fantasy and nonsense for fact leaves behind many different clues and signs that almost anyone can readily detect. Below are listed some of the most common characteristics of pseudoscience. The presence of *any one or more* of these symptoms in any material in question, marks it conclusively as pseudoscience. On the other hand, material displaying none of these flaws might still be pseudoscience – the pseudoscientists are inventing new ways to fool themselves nearly every day. What we have here is a set of *sufficient,* rather than *necessary,* conditions for pseudoscience.

The first five conditions are given here.

Pseudoscience displays an indifference to facts.

Writers tend simply to make up bogus 'facts' – what Norman Mailer calls 'factoids' – where needed, instead of going to the trouble of consulting reliable reference works, much less investigating directly. Yet these fictitious facts are often central to the pseudoscientist's argument and conclusions! This can also be seen in the fact that *pseudoscientists never revise.* The first edition of any pseudoscience book is almost always the last, even though the book may go through innumerable *new printings,* over decades or centuries. Even a book with obvious mistakes, errors, and misprints on every page is just reprinted as it is, over and over. Compare to college science textbooks, which usually see a new edition every few years because of the rapid accumulation of new facts, ideas, discoveries, experiments and insights in science.

Pseudoscience 'research' is almost invariably exegesis.

That is, the pseudoscientist clips new or old newspaper reports, collects hearsay and questionable memories, reads other pseudoscience books, or thumbs through ancient religious or mythological works. The pseudoscientist never or rarely ever makes an independent investigation to check his sources. They are taken at face value, or even better interpreted as 'symbolic', so that the pseudoscientist can use them as a kind of Rorshach inkblot – reading into the myths and old texts anything he wants to find in them. Some areas of pseudoscience are generated by very simplistic 'literalism' – the use of inherited 'sacred texts' as if they were contemporary science textbooks, a practice that leads to the flat earth, the earth at the centre of the universe, Creationism, Intelligent Design and a number of other completely foolish but resolutely traditional claims about man and nature.

Pseudoscience begins with a hypothesis – usually one that is appealing emotionally, and spectacularly implausible – and then looks only for items that appear to support it.

Conflicting evidence is ignored. Notice how often, when you are asked by a friend about what should be a question of fact if the topic were not pseudoscience, the opening phrase is, 'Do you believe in ESP?' (or flying saucers, or prophecy, or Bigfoot), not, is the evidence good, but rather, do you believe, without raising dull questions of evidence. Generally speaking, the aim of pseudoscience is to rationalize strongly held beliefs, rather than to investigate and find out what's actually going on, or to test various possibilities. Pseudoscience specializes in jumping to 'congenial conclusions', grinding ideological axes, appealing to preconceived ideas and to widespread misunderstandings. Not just Creationists, but 20th century pseudoscientists of all flavours, from J. B. Rhine and Immanuel Velikovsky to Rupert Sheldrake, have underlying their claims and assertions an anachronistic world-view that essentially rejects *all or most* of the tested, reliable findings of science.

Pseudoscience shows a total indifference to criteria of valid evidence.

The emphasis is not on meaningful, controlled, repeatable scientific experiments – instead, it is on unverifiable eyewitness testimony, stories, faked footprints, blurry photos, and tall tales, hearsay, rumour, and dubious anecdotes. Genuine modern scientific literature is not cited. Real research is never done. Generally pseudoscientists never present *any valid evidence* of any kind whatsoever for their claims. One of the most bizarre recent tactics of pseudoscientists is to publish a novel, a work of fiction in which essentially everything is made up by the author – as usual in works of fiction! – but then to turn directly around and treat the completely made-up material as if it were actual, factual and researched. Recent examples of this tactic are *The Celestine Prophecy,* by James Redfield (1994), and *The Da Vinci Code,* by Dan Brown (2003). This is really having your cake and eating it too, because the authors, when taken to task for gross errors and misstatements, calmly say, 'Can't you read? It's fiction, not non-fiction', and yet when *not* taken to task for equally gross errors, sneakily treat them as established facts and build upon them to generate yet more best-selling books.

Pseudoscience relies heavily on subjective validation.

Joe Blow puts jello on his head and his headache goes away. To pseudoscience this means jello cures headaches. To science this means nothing, since no experiment was done. Many things were going on when Joe Blow's headache went away – the moon was full, a bird flew overhead, the window was open, Joe had on his red shirt, etc. – and his headache would have gone away eventually in any case, no matter what. Modine Flark reads her newspaper horoscope and says there must be something to astrology because the horoscope describes her perfectly. But when we read it we see it is a perfectly generally true statement that describes just about every human who has ever lived, and has nothing to do with Modine or her birth-stars. These are examples of *subjective validation,* one of the main foundations of popular support for pseudoscience. Essentially all of medical quackery (aka 'alternative medicine') relies on subjective validation entirely for its continued existence. A controlled experiment to study the effectiveness of a headache remedy, for example, would put a large number – thousands or tens of thousands – of people suffering from headaches in identical circumstances, except for the presence or absence of the remedy it is desired to test, and compare the results […] which would then have some chance of being meaningful. Subjective validation renders such studies meaningless unless they follow a so-called double-blind protocol, which insures that no one involved in the study knows what the results 'should be'. That is, no one in the study should know until final results have been tabulated which patients took the remedy to be tested, and which patients took an identical-appearing placebo, known to have no effect on headaches.

We have so far been discussing pseudoscience without making any direct comparison with science itself. However, it is informative to make a direct comparison, feature by feature:

Science	Pseudoscience
The literature is written for scientists. There is peer review, and there are rigorous standards for honesty and accuracy.	The literature is aimed at the general public. There is no review, no standards, no pre-publication verification, no demand for accuracy and precision.
Reproducible, reliable results are demanded; experiments must be precisely described so that they can be duplicated exactly or improved upon in sensitivity and volume of cases or events.	Results cannot be reproduced or verified. Studies, if any, are always so vaguely described that one can't figure out just what was actually done or how it was done.
Failures are searched for and studied closely, since incorrect theories can often make correct predictions by accident but no correct theory will make incorrect predictions.	Failures are ignored, excused, hidden, lied about, discounted, explained away, rationalized, forgotten, avoided at all costs.
As time goes on, more and more is learned about the physical processes under study.	No actual physical phenomena or processes are ever found, noticed or studied. No progress is made; nothing concrete is learned.

Individual defects, idiosyncrasies and blunders of investigators average out – do not affect the real 'signal' under study.

Convinces by appeal to the evidence, by arguments based upon logical and/or mathematical reasoning, by making the best case the data permit. When new evidence contradicts old ideas, they are abandoned.

There are no conflicts of interest; the scientist has no personal financial stake in any specific outcome of his studies. (Very different from so-called 'junk science', where the self-proclaimed 'scientist' is in fact a paid employee, and paid only when he testifies to the 'right' result!)

Individual defects, idiosyncrasies and blunders of investigators provide the only 'signals' ever seen – the average is zero.

Convinces by appeal to faith and belief. Pseudoscience in almost every case has a very strong quasi-religious element: it tries to convert, not to convince. You are to believe in spite of the facts, not because of them. The original idea is never abandoned, whatever the evidence.

Extreme conflicts of interest. The pseudo-scientist generally earns some or all of his living by selling pseudoscientific 'services', e.g. horoscopes, predictions, instruction in developing paranormal powers, etc., etc.

Journalists, in particular, seem completely unable to comprehend this last point. A typical reporter asked to write an article on astrology thinks he has done a thorough job if he interviews six astrologers and one astronomer. The astronomer says it's all total bunk; the six astrologers say it's great stuff and really works and for $50 they'll be glad to cast anyone's horoscope. (No doubt!) To the reporter, and apparently to the editor and readers, this confirms astrology six to one! Yet if the reporter had had the very small degree of sense and intelligence required to realize he should have interviewed seven astronomers (all of whom are presumably knowledgeable about the planets and their interactions, but all of whom are also disinterested in astrology, and therefore able to be both knowledgeable and objective) he would have gotten the correct result: seven informed judgments that astrology is nonsense. Everything in pseudoscience seems to generate something for sale; look for courses in how to remember past lives, how to do remote viewing, how to improve your ESP ability, how to hunt for ghosts, how to become a prophet, how to heal yourself of any disease mentally, how to get the angels on your side, how to […] you name it, you got it […] but pay up first.

Comparison lists of the kind we have shown here can be continued almost indefinitely, because there is no overlap between science and pseudoscience at any point. They are precisely opposed ways of viewing nature. Science relies on, and insists on, difficult, narrow, strict procedures of self-questioning, testing and analytical thinking that make it hard to fool yourself or to avoid facing facts. Pseudoscience, on the other hand, preserves the ancient, natural, irrational, unobjective modes of thought that are tens of thousands of years older than science […] the modes of thought which have given rise to most superstition and to most of the fanciful and mistaken ideas about man and nature […] from voodoo to racism; from the flat earth to the house-shaped universe with God in the attic, Satan in the cellar and man on the ground floor; from doing rain dances to torturing and brutalizing the mentally ill to drive out the demons that possess them. Pseudoscience encourages you to believe anything you want, and supplies many examples of specious 'arguments' by which you can fool yourself into thinking your belief has some validity, despite all the facts being to the contrary. Science begins by saying, let's forget about what we *believe* to be so, and try by investigation to find out what actually *is* so. These roads don't cross; they lead in completely opposite directions.

Some confusion on this point is caused by what we might call 'crossovers'. 'Science' is not an honorary badge you wear, it's an activity you do. Whenever you cease that activity, you cease being a scientist. A distressing amount of pseudoscience is generated by actual or self-proclaimed scientists, in several ways we need to discuss. A scientist almost invariably winds up doing pseudoscience when he moves out of a field in which he is knowledgeable and competent, and plunges into another field of which he is quite ignorant. A physicist who claims to have found a new principle of biology – or a biologist who claims to have found a new principle of physics – is almost invariably doing pseudoscience. A scientist becomes a pseudoscientist when he defends an idea when all evidence and experiment is against it, because he is emotionally or ideologically committed to it. A scientist who forges data, or suppresses data that do not agree with his preconceptions, or refuses to let others see his data for independent evaluation, has become a pseudoscientist. Science is a high peak of intellectual integrity, fairness, and rationality. To carry the analogy further, the peak is slippery and smooth. It requires a tremendous effort to remain near it. But any slacking of effort carries one away, and into pseudoscience.

A fair fraction of all pseudoscience is generated by individuals who have received a small amount of very narrow and specialized scientific or technical training, but who are not professional scientists and do not comprehend the nature of the scientific enterprise – yet think of themselves as 'scientists'. Particularly notorious in this respect are medical doctors and engineers, as well as psychoanalysts and technicians of one kind or another, as well as, more recently, 'computer scientists'.

One might wonder if there are not examples of 'crossovers' in the other direction; that is people who have been thought by scientists to be doing pseudoscience, who eventually were accepted as doing valid science, and whose ideas were ultimately accepted by scientists. From what we have just outlined, one would expect this to happen extremely rarely, if ever. In fact, neither I, nor any informed colleague I have ever asked about this, knows of any single case in which this has happened during the hundreds of years the full scientific method has been known to and used by scientists. There are a large number of cases in which a scientist has been thought to be wrong by his colleagues, but whose ideas were later shown to be correct. A scientist may get a 'hunch' that some possibility is the case, without having enough evidence to convince his associates that he is correct. Such a person has not become a pseudoscientist, *unless he continues to maintain that his ideas are correct as the evidence does come in and shows conclusively that he is incorrect.* Being wrong or mistaken is unavoidable; we are all human, and we all commit errors and blunders. A scientist, however, is alert to the possibility that he might blunder, and is quick to correct mistakes, since these mistakes are completely fatal to future studies which he might undertake if they are not found and rooted out. A scientist, in short, when shown that he is mistaken by his associates, will abandon his mistaken ideas. A *pseudoscientist will not.* In fact, a short definition of pseudoscience is that it is a method for protecting and rationalizing obviously incorrect and mistaken concepts about man and nature – for excusing, defending and preserving errors.

Generally speaking, the average citizen knows as little about the history of science as he does about science itself, so it is not unusual to hear someone claim that astronomy evolved from astrology, or chemistry evolved from alchemy. Neither claim is true! In fact, calendar astronomy existed long before astrology, and no alchemist (not even Isaac Newton!) ever made any contributions to chemistry.

In one of the best review articles ever written about pseudoscience, 'Investigating the Paranormal', by David F. Marks (*Nature,* 13 March 1986), Marks summarizes psychological studies of believers in pseudoscientific concepts and concludes: 'Belief in the paranormal is metaphysical and therefore not subject to the constraints of empirically based science. [Pseudoscience] is a [...] system of untestable beliefs steeped in illusion, error and fraud. [...] Pseudosciences are remarkably stable [...] their presence on the edges of science can be expected indefinitely.' It is, unfortunately, vital for each citizen to learn to distinguish carefully between science and pseudoscience. In a democracy, every voter must be capable of seeking and recognizing authentic sources of information. Pseudoscience often strikes educated, rational people as too nonsensical and preposterous to be dangerous, a source of amusement rather than fear. Unfortunately, this is not a wise attitude. Pseudoscience can be extremely dangerous. Penetrating political systems, it has justified atrocities in the name of racial or religious purity, purging of university faculty in math and science, and interference with and discouragement of basic scientific research; penetrating the educational system, it drives out science and sensibility; penetrating the health professions it dooms thousands to unnecessary death or suffering; penetrating religion, it generates fanaticism, intolerance, and holy war; penetrating the communications media, it makes it nearly impossible for voters to obtain factual information on public issues of extreme importance – a situation which at present has reached crisis proportions in the US.

Activity 4.2

Allow 20 minutes

Identify two subjects covered in this topic that might be included under the heading 'Pseudoscience'. You may have differing views from Rory Coker (the author the material in Extract 4.5) on the definition of pseudoscience. You may also be an advocate of some of the subjects covered by Dr Coker. This diversity of view is to be encouraged; however, you should consider whether the potential problems identified by Dr Coker present a problem for you in your understanding or enthusiasm for those subjects.

Summary of Chapter 4

The ethical issues and risks associated with wild yam and St John's wort are discussed. Wild yam contains diosgenin, an example of a phytoestrogen (which are often found as phytosterols).

The relationship of phytoestrogens to cholesterol and steroid hormones in humans (especially progesterone and oestrogens) is considered in terms of their effects on the female reproductive system and assessment of risk to health (illustrating the precautionary principle).

The scientific method used to assess health (and other) risks is discussed and distinguished from pseudoscience.

Question 4.1

Contrast the risks of taking prescribed drugs derived from synthetic versions of plant compounds with the risks from natural plant formulations bought over the internet for the same medical condition.

Question 4.2

The meta-analysis study of Linde *et al.* (1996) on treatment of depression with *Hypericum* extracts reported that (from a subset of the studies) a total of 225 out of 408 people responded favourably (i.e. their symptoms reduced) to the *Hypericum* treatment, in contrast to 94 out of 420 people who responded favourably to the control (placebo) treatments. Provide a quantitative comparison of these results and discuss why individuals may have responded favourably to the control treatment.

Chapter 5

From discovery to modern medicine

To introduce the ideas of drug development, we will unravel the story of the search for a muscle relaxant from curare, which provides a fascinating insight into the conversion of local indigenous knowledge of plants to global medical application, ultimately via the development of modern drugs. It also shows how decision making about science can move from the local to the global (e.g. in the use of patents).

D

5.1 Development of drugs from curare

5.1.1 Identification of curare as a muscle relaxant for surgery

Work on the physiological effects of curare was first reported by Benjamin Collins Brodie in 1812. Brodie also collaborated with Charles Waterton on experiments with a donkey in 1814. The donkey, administered with curare, appeared to expire within 10 minutes. However, Waterton managed to revive the animal by continuous inflation of the lungs with a bellows. The donkey went on to make a full recovery, which implied that curare killed by paralysing the muscles used in breathing but the effects of smaller doses were reversible.

In 1844 the French physiologist, Claude Bernard, undertook some experiments on nerve muscle preparations from frogs and showed that the effect of curare came about by the blocking of nerve impulse transmission to the muscles. This helped confirm that the asphyxiation observed by Waterton would have been due to the paralysis of the ventilating muscles in the chest and abdomen. In 1858 the use of curare to treat tetanus was attempted. But treatment was difficult due to the inconsistency in the way that the curare was prepared and its scarcity. These

Figure 5.1 Claude Bernard (centre), a pioneer in exploring the effects of curare, working in his laboratory.

problems slowed the medical applications of curare for 80 years. In 1912 Arthur Lawen first suggested the use of curare during anaesthesia, specifically to overcome rigidity of the abdominal wall by causing the muscles to relax. Again, there was insufficient curare to test this. The first use of curare during anaesthesia was by F. P. De Caux in 1928, on seven patients at the North Middlesex Hospital in London. De Caux was unable to acquire suitable supplies of curare and his use of it lapsed. He did not publish his work, which led to his contribution being overlooked.

c

As mentioned in Chapter 3, by 1935 the active ingredient, tubocurarine, had been isolated. In 1938 Richard Gill bridged the gap between the South American rainforest and the operating theatre. Gill was inspired to collect curare because he was suffering from paralysis. Several years earlier he had been told by his doctor that he would not be able to walk nor use his hands. The diagnosis was multiple sclerosis, which Gill refused to accept, although it was confirmed at his post-mortem examination in 1958. His doctor also told him of a mysterious arrow poison called curare, which although it was one of the most deadly poisons known, had occasionally been used in modern medicine because it had a powerful muscle-relaxing effect. Gill was informed that the doctor would be willing to try curare 'if only there were enough of it in the civilised world to be standardised biologically so that safe doses could be gauged; if only it could be produced, even primitively, in batches which didn't vary in potency; if only, he kept on saying, we knew more about it'. Coincidentally, only a few months before this, Gill had been in the forests of Ecuador watching 'the witchcraft-tinctured brewing of curare' (Figure 5.2).

Figure 5.2 Curare and darts used by hunters in the Amazon forest. These items were brought back from Ecuador by Richard Gill (1901–1958).

Gill was able to bring back enough of the raw material (extracted from *Curarea*) to allow the company E. R. Squibb and Sons in 1939 to produce the first pharmaceutical product from curare, **Intocostrin** (Figure 5.3). In the preface to Gill's account of curare in his 1941 book *White Water and Black Magic* he wrote:

> Primary credit for the discovery of this drug [curare], which is at once a deadly poison and a beneficent therapeutic agent of an importance hardly second to insulin, goes to the Indians of the Amazon Basin.

c

The first published record of the use of curare in clinical anaesthesia, using Intocostrin, was by the Canadian team of Griffiths and Johnston in 1942. In the opening paragraph of their paper they stated:

> Every anaesthetist has wished at times that he might be able to produce rapid and complete muscular relaxation in resistant patients under general anaesthesia. This is a preliminary report on the clinical use of a drug which will give this kind of relaxation, temporarily and apparently quite harmlessly.

They reported on the successful use of curare extract to increase skeletal muscular relaxation in operations on 25 patients. In each case, there was rapid and complete muscular relaxation, which developed within one minute after intravenous injection and gradually disappeared after 10–15 minutes. There were no serious side-effects. It was tested in a range of operations including removal of appendix, colon or haemorrhoids, with patients ranging in age from 18 to 70.

The examples of the operations testified to the utility of the drug:

> One case was that of a man weighing 250 lbs who insisted on general anaesthesia for haemorrhoidectomy. Under cyclopropane anaesthesia, relaxation of the anal sphincter was unsatisfactory. Immediately after the administration of 5 ml of Intocostrin, compete relaxation was obtained, and the operation was easily performed.

In other cases, e.g. appendectomy, the normal situation of tensing of the abdominal muscles was avoided – within one minute of administration of Intocostrin, the abdomen was 'soft as dough'. The one drawback was the short duration of action:

> Its scope of usefulness is limited because of its somewhat fleeting action, and because it is in no sense an anaesthetic agent. It is potentially a dangerous poison, and should only be used by experienced anaesthetists in well-equipped operating rooms; but we have been so impressed by the dramatic effect produced in every one of our patients that we believe this investigation should be continued.

The scene was set for the development of muscle relaxant drugs from curare.

Figure 5.3   A poster advertising Intocostrin.

5.1.2 Patenting of curare and the development of muscle relaxant drugs

By the mid-1940s a number of applications for patents were being submitted for curare and its active ingredients. The US Patent Office granted a patent for a 'method of producing curare preparations suitable for therapeutic use' on 26 March 1946 to H. A. Holaday (working for E. R. Squibb and Son, US Patent 2397417 submitted 6 June 1941) and a second patent to J. T. Bashour on 15 October 1946, also of E. R. Squibb and Sons, New York for a 'method of producing substantially pure d-tubocurarine chloride' (US Patent 2409241, application 17 May 1944). E. R. Squibb and Sons is now Bristol Myers. These and other patents are available for viewing free online from the European Patent Office (see References and further reading) where copies of the first page of the original application are provided.

Several other patents were filed for purification of tubocurarine from curare. This was needed 'because curare [has a] low margin of safety (the range of dosage between that giving the desired skeletal-muscle effect and that giving the undesirable toxic paralysis of the muscles of respiration), [so] the physiological standardisation must be precise' (in J. T. Bashour patent description). Note how this comment echoes the doctor's comments to Gill about the risk of curare use. The final paragraph on page 1 of that submission also confirms the source of the curare as 'a crude curare syrup of non-specified botanical origin (so-called 'Gill' curare)'.

■ Are the above patents in agreement with the remit of patenting discussed in Section 2.4 where patents for inventions were defined as 'new and improved products and processes that are capable of industrial application'?

▢ Yes, because they relate to the purification and standardization of curare-derived products.

E   Could Amerindians have applied for patents of curare? Of course they would have been disadvantaged by lack of knowledge of the existence of patents! But, we have seen that they were experimenting with sources of curare and dosage. Whilst not in a formal laboratory setting, they had done much of the early curare purification. The scientists at E. R. Squibb and Sons were using Amerindian preparations of curare and not the original plants. A fair patenting system should surely include Amerindians in the early stages of the production of what was to become a global product.

The process of any drug development requires knowledge of the chemical structure of the active ingredient. Synthesising and exhaustive testing of analogues of the active ingredient follows until the very best structure is found that has an optimum effect with minimal side-effects. This expensive and lengthy process was applied to the active ingredient in Gill's curare. Following isolation and purification of tubocurarine, the plant-derived product was initially used in surgery. The structure of tubocurarine (Figure 3.4) became known only in the 1970s.

From the tubocurarine structure it was discovered that the distance of 1.15 nm (1 nm = 10^{-9} m) between the two positively charged nitrogen atoms (highlighted in Figure 3.4) was crucial to its effect. This was illustrated by the development of a synthetic analogue **decamethonium**, a relatively simple straight-chain molecule that has two positively charged nitrogen atoms the critical distance apart. (The structures of decamethonium and other compounds described in this paragraph are shown in Figure 5.4.) Decamethonium worked as an acetylcholine antagonist, like tubocurarine, but only after an initial effect as an agonist. Thus before it switched the muscle contractions off, it elicited a brief contraction. It also attached too strongly to the receptor, so its effect lasted for too long. From this product, suxamethonium was developed which has ester groups that create the spacing between the nitrogen atoms, essentially producing two joined acetylcholine molecules. The ester groups were susceptible to hydrolysis which meant that suxamethonium could be broken down in the body and become inactive. Therefore this product was fast acting with a short duration (5–10 minutes). Another line of investigation from tubocurarine led to the development of pancuronium and vecuronium in which the spacing between the nitrogen atoms was achieved with a steroid structure. These products have a higher affinity for the acetylcholine receptor sites because, like suxamethonium, they have, in effect, two acetylcholine units as part of their structure. Pancuronium and vecuronium have a long duration of action (45 minutes) with few side-effects and so became widely used. The final compound, with the most successful structure, developed through insights gained from the earlier studies on tubocurarine and suxamethonium, was **atracurium**, launched in 1983. This drug can be administered as an intravenous drip because it is rapidly broken down (hydrolysed) in the slightly alkaline environment of the blood.

Atracurium is sold today as Tracrium, a registered trademark of GlaxoSmithKline. In the UK today, synthetic analogues of curare are used in more than 50% of major operations. Overall income from the derivatives and analogues of medicinal plant products is enormous. Sales of five GlaxoSmithKline anaesthesia products including Tracrium and suxamethonium in Europe in 2003 were £69 million (although tiny compared to total GlaxoSmithKline sales of £4.85 billion in Europe in the same year). In 2003 it was reported that the two rosy periwinkle anti-cancer

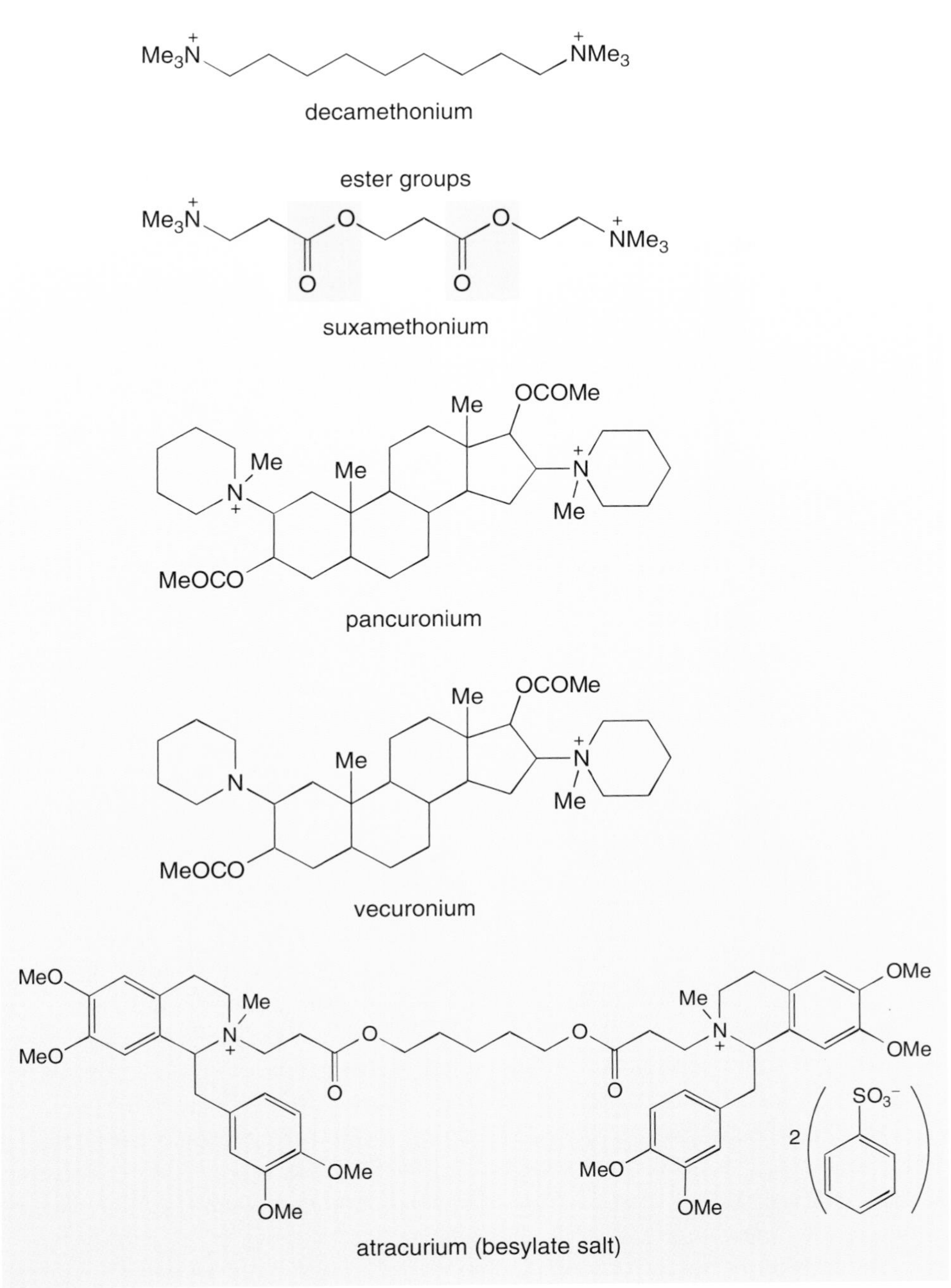

Figure 5.4 Structures of some muscle relaxant drugs.

products, vincristine and vinblastine (Section 3.1 and Figure A5.7 in the Appendix), were earning Eli Lilly $100 million annually. In most cases, there is no mechanism for feeding any of this income back to the originators of the knowledge. It can be argued that individuals are either unknown (which seems to be the case with the rosy periwinkle) or, as we discussed in Chapter 2 with respect to intellectual property rights, there are many possible recipients. However, the exploration of muscle relaxants in surgery shows that the origin and route of passage of knowledge can be determined and that directing a fraction of income back to certain Amerindian peoples might be appropriate.

5.1.3 Development of anti-malarial drugs from artemisinin

Other plant-derived drugs have followed similarly convoluted processes of development. A good example is the search for an anti-malarial drug. Malaria, spread by *Anopheles* mosquitoes and caused by protoctist parasites of the genus *Plasmodium*, is believed to be responsible for about one million deaths per year worldwide. We will not discuss the life cycle of the parasite in detail here, although you should be aware that after being introduced from an infected mosquito into its human host, the parasite develops and multiplies first in the liver and then in red blood cells. If, after this second stage of development, the infected human is bitten by another mosquito, the parasite can be transferred to that mosquito, in which it undergoes further development ready to start the cycle again.

The first plant-based anti-malarial drug was quinine (Figure A5.7 on page 93) from the bark of a South American tree in the genus *Cinchona*. The collection of the bark was organised by Jesuit priests from about 1630 onwards and the bark exported to Europe. This was an important breakthrough for Europeans as malaria was widespread in the continent in the 17th century. Eventually, in the 20th century, research on quinine analogues led to the development of a range of anti-malarial drugs, e.g. chloroquine. Quinine is believed to have an effect on a key parasite enzyme in the stages during infection of the red blood cells. There has been a continual race to develop new anti-malarial drugs as the malarial parasites have evolved resistance to existing ones. The plant *Artemisia annua*, used in Chinese medicine, has been known to have anti-malarial properties for hundreds of years. The active ingredient **artemisinin** was isolated in 1972, but its structure was not determined until 1980 (Figure 5.5a). Clinical trials of artemisinin were initially undertaken in China where, by 1979, more than 2000 cases of malaria had been cured.

The mechanism of action of artemisinin and various derivatives on malarial parasites was determined in 2003 and reported in the journal *Nature*: artemisinin disables a calcium ion pump in the cell membrane of the parasite, so disrupting the control calcium levels, leading to death of the parasite. The importance of finding a treatment for malaria was recognised in another paper in *Nature* in 2004 which described the development of a potential drug named OZ277 (Figure 5.5b) which was based on artemisinin. The development of OZ277 is summarised in Figure 5.6. The chemical details are not important; the key point is the series of changes required to derive a molecule that acts in the required way. Note that derivatives of the natural product were found to be unsuitable (Figure 5.6, lower left) and that efforts have focused on synthetic analogues. The ultimate aim, as we saw with the design of the muscle relaxant drug atracurium (Section 5.1.2), has been to generate a molecule that retains (or improves upon) the required activity, in this case as an anti-malarial agent, with minimal side-effects. As with atracurium, the molecule has to be able to reach the target area in the body, be sufficiently stable for the duration of the treatment, yet not accumulate or remain in the body beyond the treatment period. OZ277 appears to be a well designed drug based on a natural plant product which could potentially save thousands of lives; whether it will do so remains to be seen.

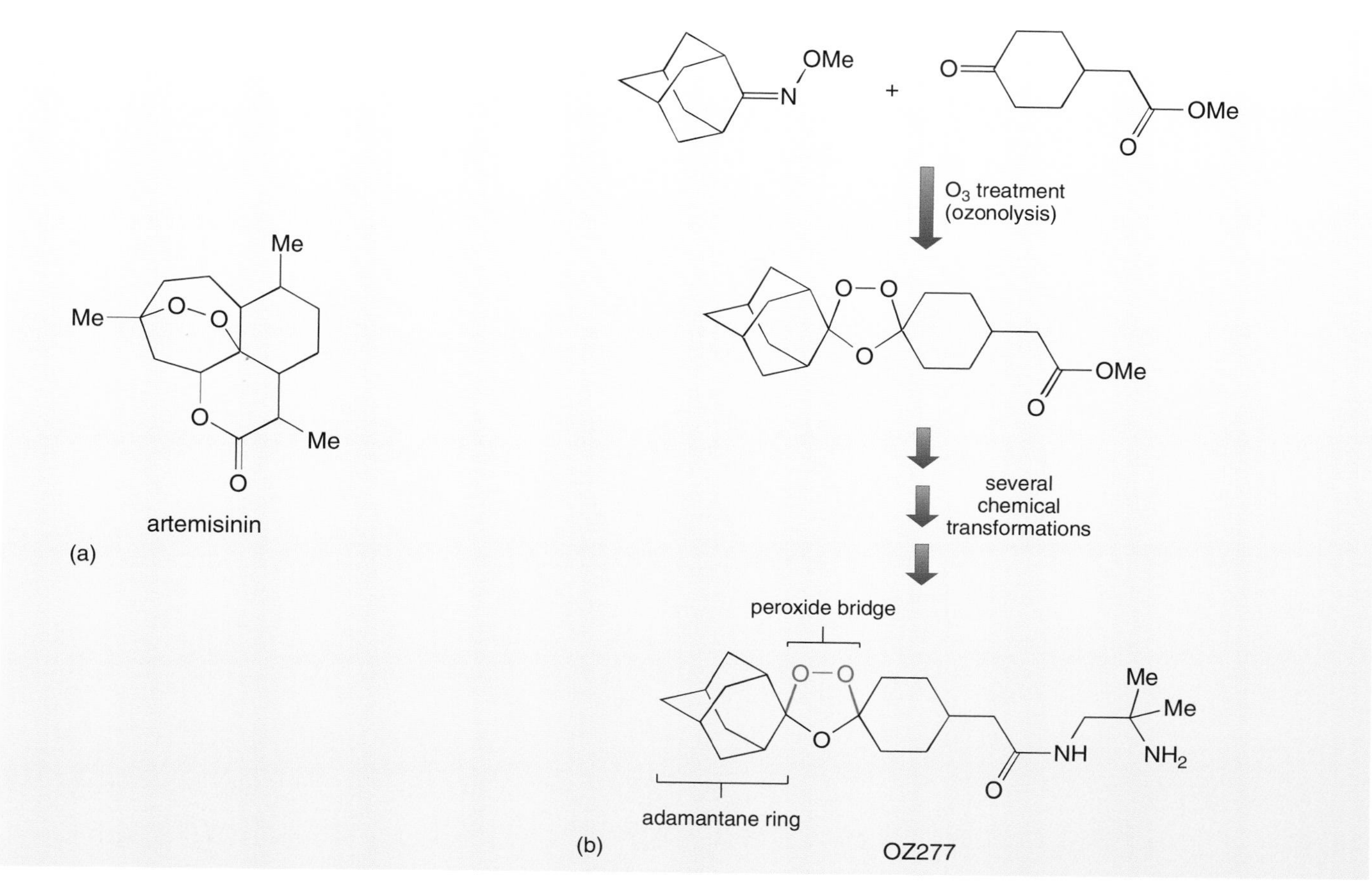

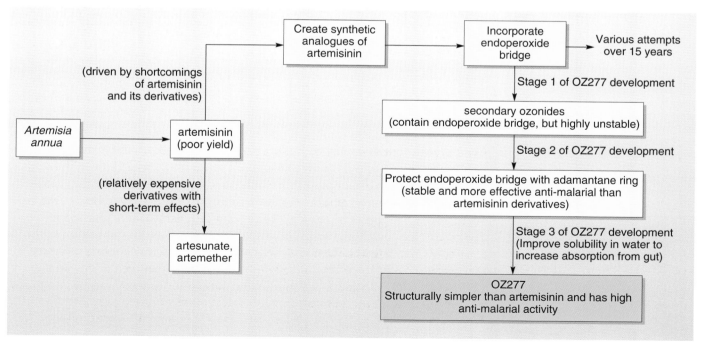

Figure 5.5 (a) Structure of artemisinin, an anti-malarial drug from *Artemisia annua*. (b) Chemical synthesis of the artemisinin analogue OZ277.

Figure 5.6 The sequence of stages in the development of OZ277.

5.2 Alkaloids and medicinal products derived from tryptophan

In this final section, we will consider how modern drug discovery can make use of information on evolutionary patterns of secondary compounds in plants. In Chapters 2, 3 and 4 we discussed how similar plants in families such as the Apiaceae and the Solanaceae can be used as sources of drugs to treat similar medical conditions. It is not just coincidental that members of these families should cure similar conditions. If plants have evolved (medicinally useful) secondary compounds as agents of defence, then we expect related plants to share these characteristics (because an ancestral characteristic is likely to be evident in species derived from that ancestor). If such patterns do exist, they may be important from a commercial perspective, allowing pharmaceutical companies to 'mine' groups of related species for active compounds, which can then be developed for drugs.

In order to explore these relationships and assess the potential of related plants as sources of medicinal products, we need to understand how medically active compounds, such as alkaloids, are synthesised by plants. Most plant alkaloids are derived from a few common amino acid origins, via a set of biosynthetic pathways. These pathways can be thought of as a manufacturing line, starting with simple ingredients (precursors), which are altered via various intermediate structures (by enzyme-catalysed reactions) to a final product, such as an alkaloid. We saw an example of a simplified biosynthetic pathway in Figure 4.3 (from cholesterol to various steroid hormones).

The biosynthetic routes by which various alkaloids are synthesised from the amino acid, **tryptophan**, are outlined in Figure 5.7 and discussed below. The important points to note are the range of medically useful products produced from these pathways (rather than details of the pathways themselves) and the relationships of the plant families in which the pathways are found. The pathways discussed here all include the intermediate **strictosidine**, from which quinine, camptothecin and various other alkaloids including ajmalicine and reserpine are synthesised (see Appendix Figure A5.7 for their structures). The medical uses of these compounds are included in Figure 5.7. We have already discussed the mechanisms of action of several of these compounds (e.g. Table 3.1).

The development of the biosynthetic pathways from the key intermediate strictosidine is associated with the evolution of the plant order Gentianales. With the exception of camptothecin (found in a plant family outside the Gentianales), all the alkaloids in Figure 5.7 are derived from members of the Gentianales. This point is made in Figure 5.8 which lists the five families in this order. Notice the large number of species in each family and the relatively small number of medicinally valuable compounds. There is no doubt that much remains to be discovered. We have to hope that the species do not go extinct first!

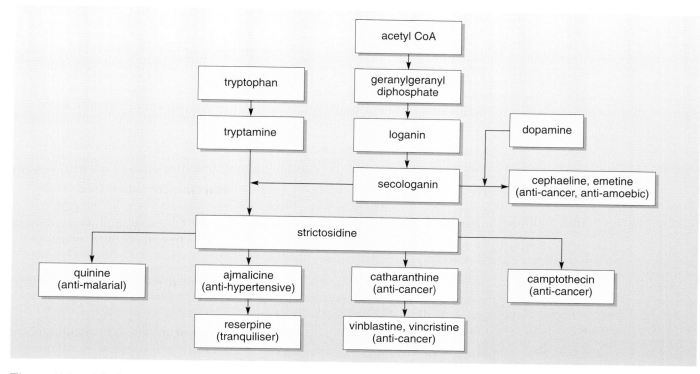

Figure 5.7 Alkaloids derived from tryptophan. Simplified biosynthetic pathways from tryptophan via a common intermediate, strictosidine, leading to various alkaloids used in medicine. (Note also the minor pathway from the strictosidine precursor secologanin.) Figure A5.7 in the Appendix shows the structures of these molecules.

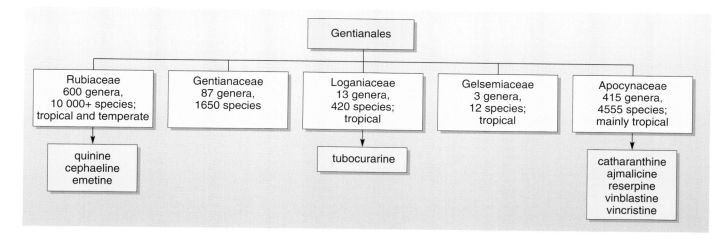

Activity 5.1

Conclusion of Activity 1.1; allow 10 minutes

As you will have seen, there are many places in the topic where risk is discussed. How did the aspects of risk discussed above match up with your expectations from Activity 1.1? Did you identify any important areas of risk that were not addressed in the text. How did the risks balance between voluntary and involuntary?

Figure 5.8 Families in the order Gentianales and some of the secondary compounds derived from them.

Summary of Chapter 5

The first hospital tests of curare as a muscle relaxant for use in surgery were made possible due to supplies of curare from Richard Gill which was developed into Intocostrin by E. R. Squibb and Sons.

Muscle relaxant drugs such as decamethonium and atracurium have been based on the structure of tubocurarine.

Anti-malarial compounds developed from artemisinin are an example of current drug development.

The exploration of compounds for drug development is helped by phylogenetic knowledge, as illustrated by the products from tryptophan (via the intermediate strictosidine) in the order Gentianales.

Question 5.1

To what extent is atracurium a laboratory product, a product of forest knowledge or a naturally occurring compound? Comment on the timescales of these three phases in the development of atracurium as a pharmaceutical product.

Question 5.2

Identify three areas of medicine discussed in this topic where knowledge of plant products has substantially improved the quality of human life or saved human life.

Conclusion

The study of medicinal plants illustrates how far science has come in understanding the natural world. We now know the molecular structure of the compounds that produce medicinal effects, the corresponding physiological processes in the human body and the reasons why the compounds evolved in plants. This knowledge has come about through both chance and the enormous efforts of many thousands of people (from herbalists to laboratory staff) driven by a desire to find cures to a wide range of diseases and conditions. Medicinal plants also allow many insights into the themes of the course. Ethical issues abound, from birth control to animal rights and sustainable harvesting to intellectual property. Oral, written and electronic communication have played major roles in the development and dissemination of the subject. Decision making has shifted from key individuals in small communities to transnational companies and governments. Finally, voluntary risk is an ongoing part of the development of medicinal plant products. Increasingly, that risk is bound up with wider information on the internet, which allows both access to formulations of plants from a global range of environments and a range of advice on the suitability or otherwise of those products. The burden of responsibility is now with us, as individuals, to assess the costs and benefits of the plant compounds that enter our bodies.

Learning Outcomes for Topic 4

The material in this topic covers many of the Learning Outcomes of the course.

The demonstration of knowledge of scientific facts, concepts and principles (Kn1) is fundamental. These include the scientific descriptions and naming of plants, the biochemical composition of medicinal plants, the physiological effects of plant compounds on the human body and the design of drugs. Scientific methodology and quantitative analysis of data (Kn2) are relevant to the design of clinical trials involving medicinal plant products and the interpretation of results. The remaining Knowledge and understanding Learning Outcomes, Kn3–Kn6, dealing with the themes of the course (communication, risk, ethical issues and decision making), are all important in this topic.

The Cognitive skill of interpreting, evaluating and synthesising scientific information (C1) is required throughout the topic. This is particularly the case where it is linked to making informed and defensible judgements about the merits of competing views (C3). This is developed in Chapter 4 where contrasting claims about wild yam and St John's wort are discussed. The other Cognitive skills (C2, C4 and possibly C5) are equally relevant.

Ky1 and Ky4 (i.e. working with relevant information and communicating information appropriately) are clearly important in this topic, although there is less emphasis on data handling, numeracy and mathematics (Ky2, Ky3) than in other topics. There may be opportunities to develop your skills of working with others (Ky5) and you should continually strive to become a more effective learner (Ky6).

Answers to questions

Question 2.1

Medicinal plant properties were initially conveyed orally from one person to either one or a few others, possibly restricted to a local community. Knowledge of the properties may have been passed down the generations from one person to one other. The written herbals heralded a wider audience and allowed one person to reach a much larger audience over many years. The herbals may have been updated/edited/translated by later writers who either added supplementary information or altered the text (perhaps unwittingly). In the last 100 years the properties of medicinal plants have been reported in the scientific literature, potentially restricting access to a narrow specialist audience. However, books such as those by Waterton helped spread information about medicinal plants to a wider audience. Finally, the Internet has opened up communication, allowing many people to access specialist scientific literature/research alongside other types of sources, which vary in reliability. Conversely, anybody can potentially place information on the web, leading to the largest possible multi-way communication on medicinal plants (or any other subject area). Furthermore, such information can be updated much more rapidly than is possible with conventional printed texts.

Question 3.1

Examples include curare derivatives, morphine and atropine. The active secondary compounds have evolved to aid plant defence against a variety of potential natural enemies. This may be directly beneficial to humans because the plant secondary compound kills pathogens that also invade humans (e.g. malarial parasites) or halts unwanted cellular proliferations in the body (i.e. cancer). Indirect benefits accrue because humans can alter the site, dosage or structure of the compound and thereby ensure that harmful effects (e.g. on muscle relaxation) are at an acceptable level.

Question 4.1

The main difference between risks of prescribed drugs and risks of natural plant formulations are the unknown aspects of the latter. This may be due to the main ingredient or secondary ingredients. Risks from prescribed drugs are usually well known and described and can be discussed with the medical practitioner or pharmacist issuing the drugs. There may be information associated with the natural plant formulations but the user is required to assess and interpret those risks. Of course, there may be side-effects with any prescription because of the variation in physiological responses of patients.

Question 4.2

The data can be summarised as the fraction of people responding favourably to the *Hypericum* extract ($225/408 = 0.552$ or 55.2%) compared with the fraction of people responding favourably to the control ($94/420 = 0.224$ or 22.4%). Thus the fraction of people responding favourably to the extract was more than twice as high as the fraction responding to the control. If you are familiar with statistics, you may note that these data could be compared with a chi-squared (or G) test.

The reasons why people may respond favourably to the placebo are threefold. First, it may be that they are not actually responding to the placebo but simply recovering by themselves. Second, because we are dealing with depression, it may be that the people respond to the placebo because they believe it is a useful drug. Third, it is possible (though unlikely) that the placebo contains something that causes the patient to recover. The latter may either be a medical breakthrough or a poorly designed clinical trial!

Question 5.1

The forerunners of atracurium were the natural plant products such as tubocurarine with related chemical structures. The forest knowledge allowed the plants containing those compounds to be identified and selected from all the other possible forest plants. The study of the molecular structure and chemical properties of atracurium's predecessors allowed the fine-tuning that led to the synthesis of the final products. The first stage of development (in the plant) occurred over millions of years, the second stage (between forest people and their environment) occurred over hundreds or possibly several thousand years. The final stage took place over less than 40 years (from Intocostrin to atracurium); in fact, the conclusion of this stage, i.e. from the discovery of the structure of tubocurarine to the commercial production of atracurium, took less than a decade.

Question 5.2

There are several areas of medicine that relate to material in this topic: anti-cancer therapies, especially taxol from *Taxus* species and vinblastine or vincristine from *Catharanthus*; muscle relaxants in surgery, specifically curare-derived products and anti-malarials, including quinine and now artemisinin. Other examples include painkillers such as morphine and aspirin.

Comments on activities

Activity 1.1

See the comments under Activity 5.1 when you have completed this activity.

Activity 1.2

There are no comments on this activity.

Activity 1.3

The increasing number of medicinal plants harvested from the wild, coupled with unsustainable harvesting practices, is leading to reductions in medicinal plant populations. The pressures on these populations are fuelled by an increase in global demand of about 10% per year over a 10-year period. The world market in 2004 was estimated at £11 billion. (Another estimate from a different source gave a world value of $43 billion in 2000.)

Activity 4.1

(a) Extract 4.1 is mostly impersonal, presenting a set of statements about either the product or its use. This contrasts with Extract 4.2 which is based on the experiences of one individual with a strong personal account of physical and emotional difficulties and how these have largely been removed by the application of a wild yam product. The style changes a little when the personal experiences are supported by scientific statements from a named source.

Extract 4.1 refers to unnamed sources to support its statements:

> There is no sound scientific evidence to indicate [...] In studies done so far, a dummy cream worked just as well.

Extract 4.2 has conflicting commercial interests. The author of the testimonial refers to her own company. The whole testimonial is embedded within a larger website supported by an organisation with commercial interests. The author also describes the work of Dr Betty Kamen (and her book), yet no other source, which suggests that the book is being advertised. (You will see that Dr Kamen is also mentioned in relation to wild yam in Extract 4.3, from the Quackwatch website.)

(b) There are two important inconsistencies in the extracts. Extract 4.1 states that wild yam does not contain progesterone whilst Extract 4.2 describes 'a natural form of progesterone made from a wild Mexican yam'. The second inconsistency concerns the effect of wild yam on hormonal levels. Both extracts agree that wild yam may help relax muscles, reducing menstrual cramping (note that Extract 4.1 refers to alkaloid content of wild yam), and may have other beneficial effects. Extract 4.2 describes a range of benefits including removal or dramatic reduction of symptoms of premenstrual syndrome. (It is worth noting that wild yam creams may contain a large number of ingredients, many of which are plant-based, with no indication of quantity.) These statements are contradicted in Extract 4.1, which states that 'there is no sound scientific evidence to indicate that rubbing wild yam cream into the belly, thighs, or any other soft areas will relieve symptoms of premenstrual syndrome (PMS) or menopause'.

(You may wish to explore Extracts 4.1 and 4.2 in more detail by following the web addresses given in the References and further reading section. You may also wish to search on 'wild yam' on the internet to check the details given about products.)

Activity 4.2

The Doctrine of Signatures and the early communication of knowledge through herbals are two candidates for pseudoscience. The first relies on supposed links between the structure and function of the plant and human illness. It also relies on the interpretations of one or two individuals and communication by an unknown creative force. The second may have used hearsay and anecdote (sometimes based on the Doctrine of Signatures) to assemble a set of medicinal plants. The problem with a simple judgement of these two subjects as pseudoscience is that the set of plants also includes some potentially useful members, which have benefited humans and been shown to contain medicinally useful compounds. Thus we have to be careful in sifting through the literature on medicinal plants to ensure that not all of them are rejected on the basis of their association with pseudoscience.

Activity 5.1

The estimation of risk was discussed with respect to HRT and St John's wort. Whilst more detailed scientific studies help to identify the causes and magnitude of risk to human health, we are still left with various uncertainties. These may occur for reasons including the following:

- variation of effects of plant products with dosage and site of application
- the possible effects of other compounds present in the medicinal product
- unexpected interactions between human biochemistry/physiology and the introduced compounds (i.e. side-effects), independently of genetic variation
- genetic variation between humans.

The nature of the voluntary risk associated with modern usage of medicinal plant products was also highlighted, particularly in relation to the use of plant extracts that affect the female reproductive system and those that are used to treat mild depression.

References and further reading

Angiosperm phylogeny group website: http://www.mobot.org/MOBOT/research/APweb/welcome.html (accessed October 2005).

Bisset, N. G. (1992). War and hunting poisons of the New World, Part 1: Notes on the early history of curare, *Journal of Ethnopharmacology*, **36**, pp. 1–26.

Blamey, M. and Grey-Wilson, C. (1989) *The Illustrated Flora of Britain and Northern Europe*, Hodder & Stoughton, London.

Clapham, A. L., Tutin, T. G. and Warburg, E. F. (1981) *Excursion Flora of the British Isles*, 3rd edn, Cambridge University Press.

Eckstein-Ludwig, U. *et al.* (2003) Artemisinins target the SERCA of *Plasmodium falciparum*, *Nature*, **424**, pp. 957–961.

European Patent Office at: http://www.european-patent-office.org/index.en.php (accessed October 2005).

Fisher, N. (1996) *Classics Ireland*, vol. 3. ISSN 0791–9417. Classical Association of Ireland. http://www.ucd.ie/classics/classicsinfo/ClassicsIreland.html (accessed December 2005).

Gerard, J. (1636) *Gerard's Herball*, T. H. Johnston (Ed.). Reduced version edited by Marcus Woodward (1927). Reprinted by Bracken Books (1985).

Gill, R. C. (1941) *White Water and Black Magic*, Victor Gollancz Ltd, London.

Government-backed home page of UK Intellectual Property on the Internet at: http://www.intellectual-property.gov.uk (accessed October 2005).

Griffiths, H. R. (1951) The evolution of use of curare in anaesthesiology, *Annals of the New York Academy of Sciences*, **54**, pp. 493–497.

Griffiths, H. R. and Johnston, G. E. (1942) The use of curare in general anaesthesia, *Anaesthesiology*, **3**, pp. 418–420.

Harborne, J. B. (1993) *Introduction to Ecological Biochemistry* (4th edn), Academic Press, New York. [Demonstrates clearly the link between secondary chemicals in plant defence and their potential effects on humans.]

Hubbard, T. (2004) We're patently going mad, *The Guardian*, 4 March 2004, Guardian Unlimited: Science.

Hypericum Depression Trial Study Group, *Journal of the American Medical Association*, 2002. Source: National Center for Complementary and Alternative Medicine (NCCAM) fact sheet.

Julien, R. M. (1995) *A Primer of Drug Action*, W. H. Freeman and Company, New York. [Good mixture of biochemical and physiological detail with information on drug groups and products.]

Linde, K., Ramirez, G., Mulrow, C.D. *et al.* (1996) St John's wort for depression – an overview and meta-analysis of randomised clinical trials, *British Medical Journal*, **313**, pp. 253–258.

MacLatchy, D. L. and Van Der Kraak, G. J. (1995) The phytoestrogen β-sitosterol alters the reproductive endocrine status of goldfish, *Toxicology and Applied Pharmacology*, **134**, pp. 305–312.

Mann, J. (2000) *Murder, Magic and Medicine*, Oxford University Press. [A highly readable guide to many of the plant-based drugs discussed in this topic; especially relevant are sections on anti-cancer, anti-malarial and effects on the reproductive system.]

Norfolk and Waveney Mental Health Partnership website, for St John's wort, at: http://www.nmhct.nhs.uk/pharmacy/stjohnswort.htm (accessed October 2005).

Patrick, G. L. (2001) *An Introduction to Medicinal Chemistry*, Oxford University Press. [Accessible and comprehensive coverage of many of the biochemical structures and functions described in this topic.]

Petrucelli, J. D., Nandram, B. and Chen, M. (1999) *Applied Statistics for Engineers and Scientists*, Prentice Hall, New Jersey.

Rang, H. P., Dale, M. M. and Ritter, J. M. (1999) *Pharmacology* (4th edn), Churchill Livingstone, London.

Roth, W. E. (1922–3) (Trans. and Ed.) *Richard Schomburgk's Travels in British Guiana (1840–1844)*, National Museum, Georgetown, British Guiana.

Shelton, R. C., Keller, M. B., Gelenberg, A. *et al.* (2001) Effectiveness of St John's wort in major depression: a randomized controlled trial, *Journal of the American Medical Association*, **285**, pp. 1978–1986.

Shiva, V. (2003) *Biodiversity, Biotechnology and Intellectual Property Rights: Globalisation and Emerging Determinants of Public Health*, http://www.movement.org.uk/clientsuppliedfiles/biodiversity.pdf (accessed December 2005).

Stenton, G. (2003) Biopiracy within the pharmaceutical industry, *Hertfordshire Law Journal*, **1**, pp. 30–47.

Stevens, J. E. (1973) *Discovering Wild Plant Names*, Shire Publications Ltd, Aylesbury.

Tatman, J., *Silphium: ancient wonder drug?*, at: http://ancient-coins.com/articles/silphium/silphium2.htm (accessed October 2005).

Watson, P. (1983) This precious foliage: a study of the aboriginal psychoactive drug pituri, *Oceania Monograph* No. **26**, Oceania publications, University of Sydney Press.

Watson, R., Luanratana, O. and Griffin, W. J. (1983) The ethnopharmacology of pituri, *Journal of Ethnopharmacology*, **8**, pp. 303–311.

Sources of Extracts 4.1–4.5

Extract 4.1

From: http://www.wholehealthmd.com/refshelf/substances_view/ 1,1525,10070,00.html (accessed October 2005).

Extract 4.2

From: http://www.all-natural.com/wildyam.html (accessed October 2005), http://www.all-natural.com/ and the linked page: http://www.all-natural.com/ herbguid/html (accessed October 2005).

Extract 4.3

From: http://www.quackwatch.org/01QuackeryRelatedTopics/wildyam.html (accessed October 2005).

Extract 4.4

From: http://www.mind.org.uk/Information/Factsheets/ Treatments+and+drugs/St+Johns+Wort++-+Hypericum+perforatum.htm (accessed October 2005).

Extract 4.5

From: http://www.quackwatch.org/01QuackeryRelatedTopics/pseudo.html (accessed October 2005).

Acknowledgements

Grateful acknowledgement is made to the following sources for permission to reproduce material within this book:

Text

Extract 1.1: Edwards, R. (2004) No remedy insight for herbal ransack, *New Scientist*, 10 January 2004; *Extract 4.*1: Copyright © www.wholehealthmd.com; *Extract 4.3*: By permission of Timothy N. Gorski; *Extract 4.4*: St John's wort – *Hypericum perforatum*, September 2002. Copyright © MIND, www.mind.org.uk/information; *Extract 4.5*: By permission of Rory Coker.

Figures

Figure 1.2a: Copyright © Silvio Fiore/Topfoto.co.uk; *Figure 1.5*: Copyright © Dan Sams/Science Photo Library; *Figure 1.7a*: Courtesy of The Medicinal Plant Specialist Group of the Species Survival Commission, IUCN–The World Conservation Union; *Figure 1.7b*: From www.nakaherbs.com; *Figure 2.1a*: Copyright © Gail Jankus/Science Photo Library; *Figure 2.1b*: Forest and Kim Starr (USGS); *Figures 2.3, 2.4*: Mary Evans Picture Library; *Figures 2.5, 3.8*: Copyright © Michael Gillman; *Figure 2.9*: Blamey, M. and Grey-Wilson, C. (1989) *The Illustrated Flora of Britain and Northern Europe*, Hodder & Stoughton. Copyright © Marjorie Blamey 1989; *Figure 2.10a*: Copyright © Adrian Thomas/Science Photo Library; *Figure 2.10b*: Copyright © Anthony Cooper/Science Photo Library; *Figure 2.10c, d*: Copyright © Sheila Terry/ Science Photo Library; *Figure 4.1*: Copyright © Natural History Museum; *Figure 4.6*: St John's wort packaging; *Figure 5.1*: Copyright © Jean-Loup Charmet/Science Photo Library; *Figure 5.2*: American Society of Anesthesiologists; *Figure 5.5* is adapted from two figures by Yarnell, A. (2004) 'Malaria drug design on a dime', *Medicinal Chemistry*, vol. 82, no. 34, American Chemical Society.

Every effort has been made to contact copyright holders. If any have been inadvertently overlooked, the publishers will be pleased to make the necessary arrangements at the first opportunity.

Figure A3.1 (*opposite*) Structures of compounds named in Figure 3.1.

Appendix

ISOPRENOIDS

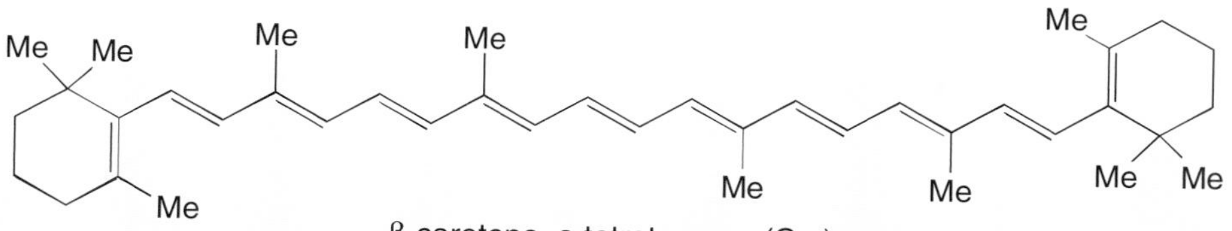

β-carotene, a tetraterpene (C_{40})

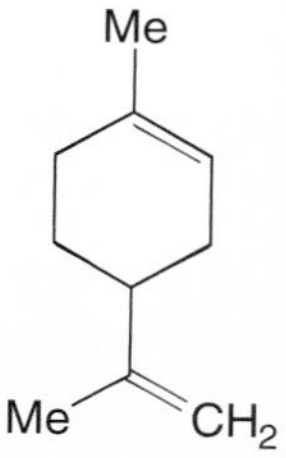

limonene
(a terpene)

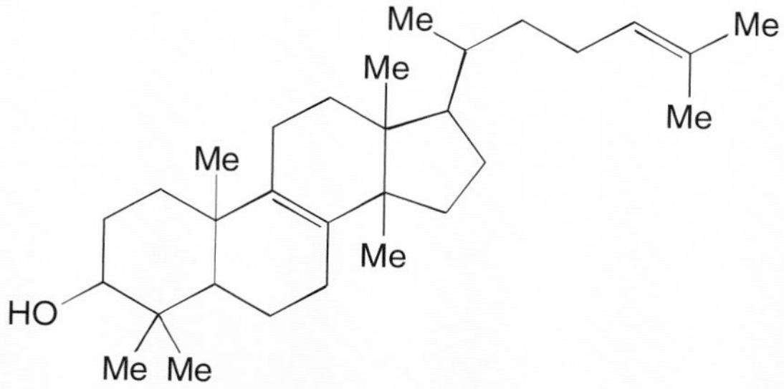

lanosterol, a triterpene (C_{30})

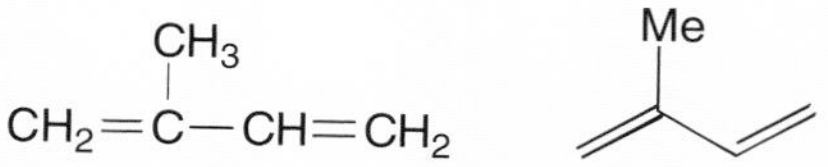

$$CH_2{=}C{-}CH{=}CH_2$$

isoprene

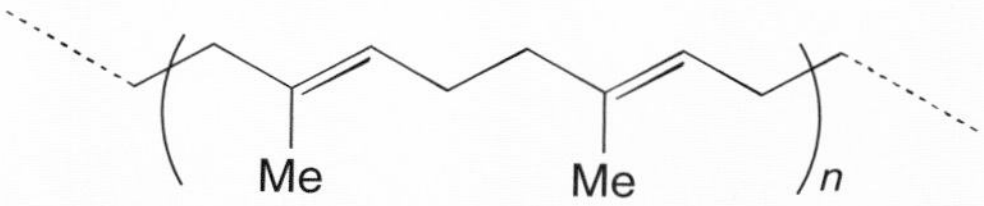

polyisoprene

FLAVONOIDS

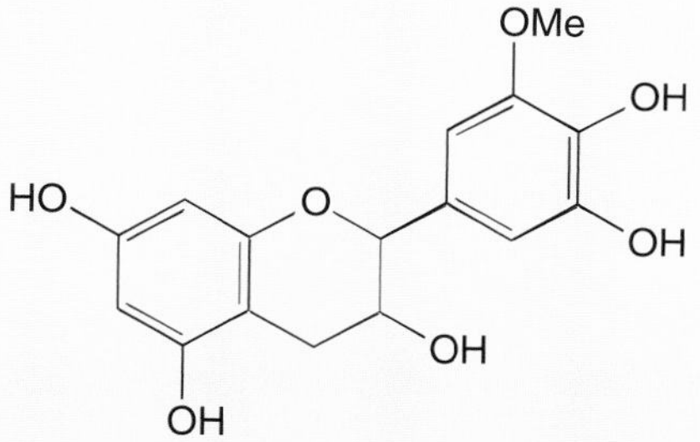

petunidin (a flavonoid flower pigment)

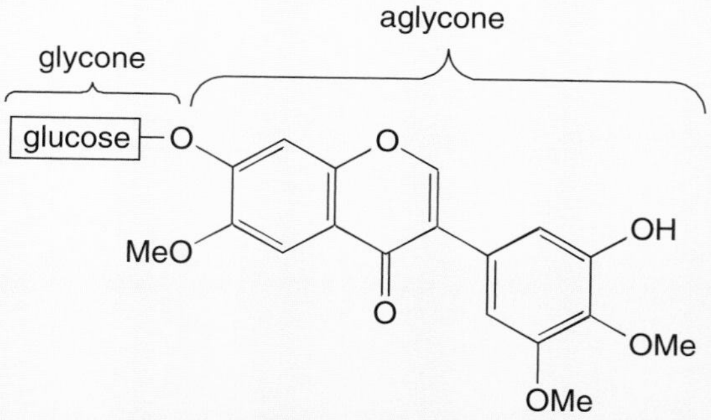

glycone

aglycone

glucose

iridin (an isoflavone glycoside from iris flowers)

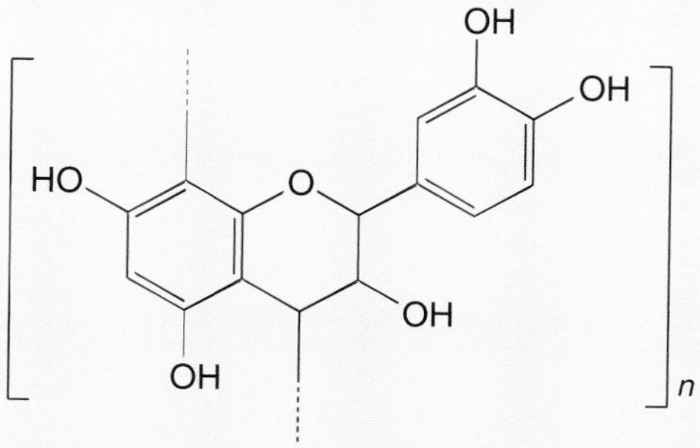

a tannin
(structure of repeating unit)

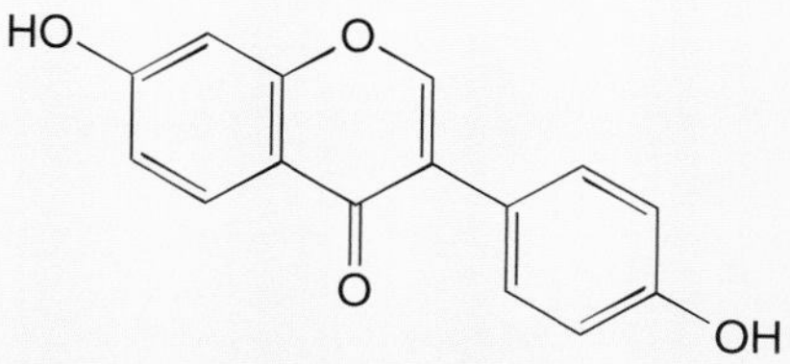

daidzein (an isoflavone)

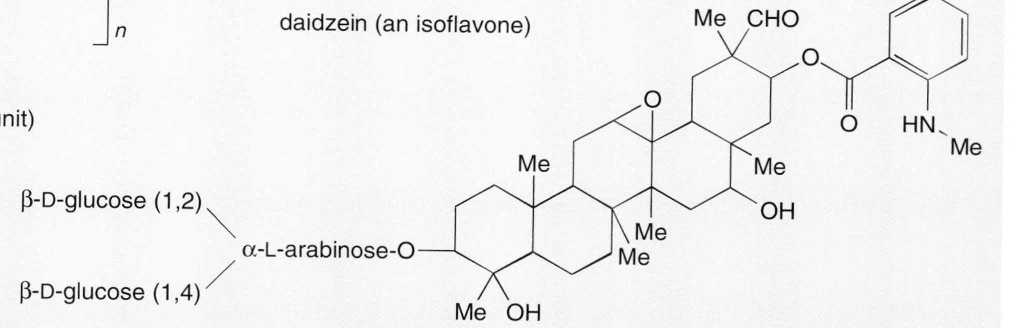

β-D-glucose (1,2)
α-L-arabinose-O
β-D-glucose (1,4)

a saponin (avenacin A from oat roots)

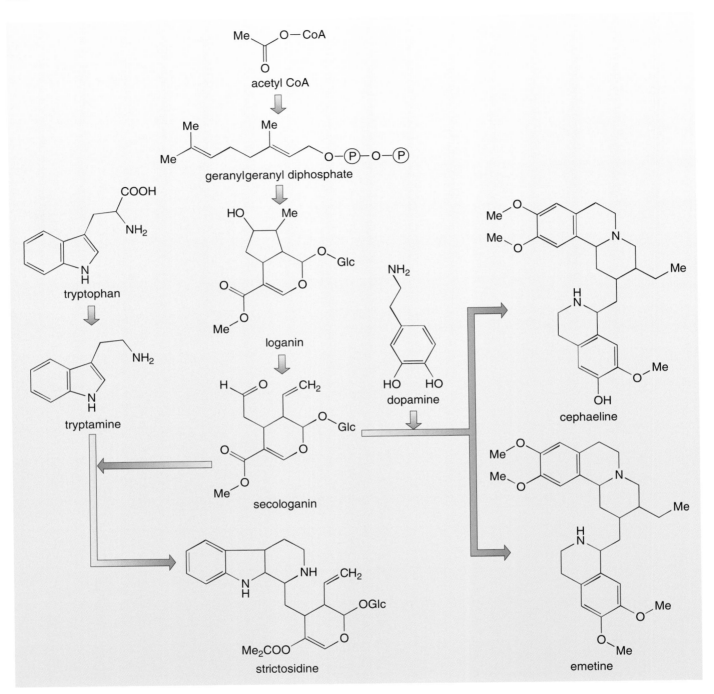

Figure A5.7 (*Part 1*) Structures of and biosynthetic relationships between compounds named in Figure 5.7. (Glc = glucose)

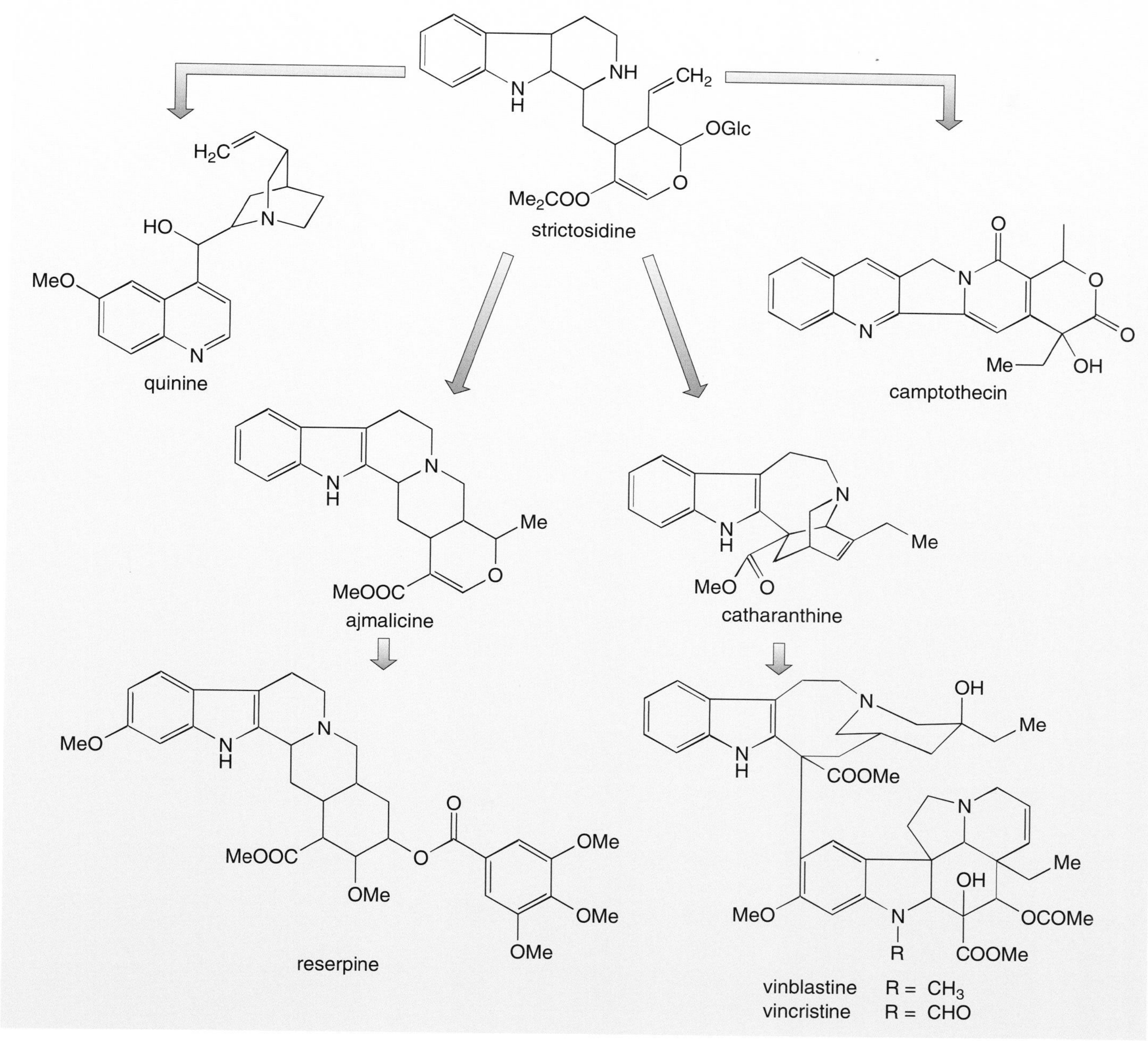

Figure A5.7 (*Part 2*) Structures of and biosynthetic relationships between compounds named in Figure 5.7.

Index

Entries and page numbers in **bold** refer to terms that are printed in **bold** in the text and defined in the Glossary. Page numbers referring to figures and tables are printed in *italics*.